"Before the 'New Atheism,' [...] Richard Dawkins as an anachronism—a devotee to a hyper-authoritarian, hyper-reductionist kind of science worship that rose and fell in rough unison with the Soviet Union. Instead, he reminds us that in an age when so many are creating gods after their own image, atheism will always have some appeal. With great care and kindness, Ransom Poythress reveals the Dawkins deception for what it is, offering practical ways to dialogue with people who have come under its spell."

—**Douglas Axe**, Author, *Undeniable: How Biology Confirms Our Intuition That Life Is Designed*

"Do we really need yet one more critique of Richard Dawkins and the 'New Atheists'? When you have read this splendid volume, you will have no doubts: we do, and this one fills a need not yet filled. Poythress examines the dilemma often presented—Christian faith or science—and says, no: it's Christian faith and good science, or, better, good science because of Christian faith. While he interacts with the scientistic claims made by doctrinaire evolutionists (Poythress is a trained biologist), the book goes far beyond, and explores the historical, psychological, and spiritual reasons that draw people to atheism. And then even beyond that, the book presents the Christian alternative in a winsome and convincing manner. It deserves a wide readership, both by scientists and by laypersons."

—**William Edgar**, Professor of Apologetics, Westminster Theological Seminary, Philadelphia

"The 'New Atheists' have terrorized many Christians by invoking modern science and philosophy to debunk Jesus and the Bible. Richard Dawkins has been one of their most effective voices, focusing especially on the doctrine of evolution, which most academic and media writers assume to be true. Ransom Poythress is well qualified to respond to Dawkins and more generally to the New Atheist movement. He writes knowledgeably about evolution, science, philosophy, and theology, devastating the arguments and conclusions of the New Atheists. His presentation is powerful, but also gracious and winsome. I recommend this book to anyone who seeks knowledge of these issues and reliable guidance through the conceptual thicket."

—**John M. Frame**, Professor of Systematic Theology and Philosophy Emeritus, Reformed Theological Seminary

"The New Atheism is now an established feature of the intellectual landscape of our age. Richard Dawkins was one of the chief architects and intellectuals of the New Atheists. Ransom Poythress has written an accessible introduction to Dawkins's life and thought and a compelling refutation of his arguments against Christianity. This is an enormously helpful resource."

—**R. Albert Mohler Jr.**, President, The Southern Baptist Theological Seminary

Praise for the Great Thinkers Series

"After a long eclipse, intellectual history is back. We are becoming aware, once again, that ideas have consequences. The importance of P&R Publishing's leadership in this trend cannot be overstated. The series Great Thinkers: Critical Studies of Minds That Shape Us is a tool that I wish I had possessed when I was in college and early in my ministry. The scholars examined in this well-chosen group have shaped our minds and habits more than we know. Though succinct, each volume is rich, and displays a balance between what Christians ought to value and what they ought to reject. This is one of the happiest publishing events in a long time."

—**William Edgar**, Professor of Apologetics, Westminster Theological Seminary

"When I was beginning my studies of theology and philosophy during the 1950s and '60s, I profited enormously from P&R's Modern Thinkers Series. Here were relatively short books on important philosophers and theologians such as Nietzsche, Dewey, Van Til, Barth, and Bultmann, by scholars of Reformed conviction such as Clark, Van Riessen, Ridderbos, Polman, and Zuidema. These books did not merely summarize the work of these thinkers; they were serious critical interactions. Today, P&R is resuming and updating the series, now called Great Thinkers. The new books, on people such as Aquinas, Hume, Nietzsche, Derrida, and Foucault, are written by scholars who are experts on these writers. As before, these books are short—around 100 pages. They set forth accurately the views of the thinkers under consideration, and they enter into constructive dialogue, governed by biblical and Reformed convictions. I look forward to the release of all the books being planned and to the good influence they will have on the next generation of philosophers and theologians."

—**John M. Frame**, Professor of Systematic Theology and Philosophy Emeritus, Reformed Theological Seminary, Orlando

Richard

DAWKINS

GREAT THINKERS

A Series

Series Editor
Nathan D. Shannon

AVAILABLE IN THE GREAT THINKERS SERIES

Thomas Aquinas, by K. Scott Oliphint
Richard Dawkins, by Ransom Poythress
Jacques Derrida, by Christopher Watkin
Michel Foucault, by Christopher Watkin
G. W. F. Hegel, by Shao Kai Tseng
Karl Marx, by William D. Dennison

FORTHCOMING

Francis Bacon, by David C. Innes
Karl Barth, by Lane G. Tipton
David Hume, by James N. Anderson
Friedrich Nietzsche, by Carl R. Trueman
Karl Rahner, by Camden M. Bucey
Adam Smith, by Jan van Vliet

Richard

DAWKINS

Ransom Poythress

P&R
P U B L I S H I N G
P.O. BOX 817 • PHILLIPSBURG • NEW JERSEY 08865-0817

Scripture quotations are from The Holy Bible, English Standard Version, copyright © 2001 by Crossway, a publishing ministry of Good News Publishers. Used by permission. All rights reserved. All quotations are from the 2011 text edition of the ESV.

Italics within Scripture quotations indicate emphasis added.

ISBN: 978-1-62995-221-5 (pbk)
ISBN: 978-1-62995-222-2 (ePub)
ISBN: 978-1-62995-223-9 (Mobi)

Printed in the United States of America

Library of Congress Cataloging-in-Publication Data

Names: Poythress, Ransom, author.
Title: Richard Dawkins / Ransom Poythress.
Description: Phillipsburg NJ : Ransom Poythress, [2018] | Series: Great
  thinkers | Includes bibliographical references and index.
Identifiers: LCCN 2018023061| ISBN 9781629952215 (pbk.) | ISBN
  9781629952222 (epub) | ISBN 9781629952239 (mobi)
Subjects: LCSH: Dawkins, Richard, 1941- | Christianity and atheism. | God. |
  Atheism. | Reformed Church--Doctrines.
Classification: LCC BR128.A8 P69 2018 | DDC 261.2/1--dc23
LC record available at https://lccn.loc.gov/2018023061

To the glory of God,
and to my parents,
who taught me to appreciate God's glory
as revealed in Scripture and creation

CONTENTS

SERIES INTRODUCTION

Amid the rise and fall of nations and civilizations, the influence of a few great minds has been profound. Some of these remain relatively obscure, even as their thought shapes our world; others have become household names. As we engage our cultural and social contexts as ambassadors and witnesses for Christ, we must identify and test against the Word those thinkers who have so singularly formed the present age.

The Great Thinkers series is designed to meet the need for critically assessing the seminal thoughts of these thinkers. Great Thinkers hosts a colorful roster of authors analyzing primary source material against a background of historical contextual issues, and providing rich theological assessment and response from a Reformed perspective.

Each author was invited to meet a threefold goal, so that each Great Thinkers volume is, first, *academically informed*. The brevity of Great Thinkers volumes sets a premium on each author's command of the subject matter and on the secondary discussions that have shaped each thinker's influence. Our authors identify the most influential features of their thinkers' work and address them with precision and insight. Second, the series maintains a high standard of *biblical and theological faithfulness*. Each volume stands on an epistemic commitment to "the whole counsel of God" (Acts 20:27), and is thereby equipped for fruitful critical engagement. Finally, Great Thinkers texts are *accessible*, not burdened with jargon or unnecessarily difficult vocabulary. The goal is to inform and equip the reader as effectively as possible through clear writing, relevant analysis, and incisive, constructive critique. My hope is that this series will distinguish itself by striking with biblical faithfulness and the riches of the Reformed tradition at the central nerves of culture, cultural history, and intellectual heritage.

Bryce Craig, president of P&R Publishing, deserves hearty thanks for his initiative and encouragement in setting the series in motion and seeing it through. Many thanks as well to P&R's director of academic development, John Hughes, who has assumed, with cool efficiency, nearly every role on the production side of each volume. The Rev. Mark Moser carried much of the burden in the initial design of the series, acquisitions, and editing of the first several volumes. And the expert participation of Amanda Martin, P&R's editorial director, was essential at every turn. I have long admired P&R Publishing's commitment, steadfast now for over eighty-five years, to publishing excellent books promoting biblical understanding and cultural awareness, especially in the area of Christian apologetics. Sincere thanks to P&R, to these fine brothers and sisters, and to several others not mentioned here for the opportunity to serve as editor of the Great Thinkers series.

Nathan D. Shannon
Seoul, Korea

FOREWORD

Even though Richard Dawkins's star may no longer be in the ascendant, his influence, particularly in generating an antitheistic attitude among young people, is still sufficiently pervasive to merit the consideration given to it in this short and accessible book. Poythress provides the reader with a clear map of the so-called New Atheist belief system to which Dawkins is committed and explains why its narrative appeals to so many people.

The author then dives beneath the surface and subjects that narrative in a fair and intelligible way to an intense yet fair and thoughtful scrutiny. He illuminates its factual falsehoods, illogical statements, inconsistencies, and failings in the handling of evidence with the result that the reader is left with a clear idea why atheism is not the only possible viewpoint for an intelligent, literate person to hold. A particularly helpful feature of the book is the practical guidelines it gives for entering into discussion with atheists.

Dawkins's attempts to use the cultural authority of science to deny the existence of God met with a strong and entirely justified response. Indeed, it could be argued that Dawkins may deter young people from studying science by saying that science and God do not mix, when the history of modern science shows the exact opposite—that far from belief in God hindering science, it was the motor that drove it. Poythress's discussion of science and God forms an important antidote to Dawkins's scientism, as well as his failure to come to grips with the nature of God in any sensible way.

I welcome and recommend Poythress's book and trust that it will not only inform people but give them the courage to get involved in the debate themselves.

John C. Lennox
Emeritus Professor of Mathematics
Emeritus Fellow in Mathematics and Philosophy of Science
Green Templeton College
University of Oxford

ACKNOWLEDGMENTS

This work would not have been possible without the support and encouragement of a loving, caring community of people. I would like to thank David Garner, John Hughes, Mark Moser, Nate Shannon, Jim Scott, and the support staff at P&R Publishing for working with me through the development and production of this manuscript. I would also like to thank the individuals who gave so generously of their time and energy in lending me their editorial and theoretical expertise in reviewing drafts of this document: Vern, Diane, and Justin Poythress, Jay and Carolyn Castelli, Phil Welch, and my colleagues Benjamin Lipscomb and James Wolfe. I would like to especially thank the brightest star in my life, my wife, Lisbeth, for her patience, kindness, wisdom, love, insight, and relentless encouragement all through this project. Most importantly, I want to thank and glorify my Creator, God. May he continue to use me as a worker to bring in the harvest he has prepared.

INTRODUCTION

WHO IS RICHARD DAWKINS, AND WHY IS HE IMPORTANT?

This short volume seeks to equip lay readers with a brief historical and cultural context, as well as an understanding of the major
themes, arguments, and flaws in Richard Dawkins's thinking.
Additionally, I want to make a positive, strategic case for how
Christians can confidently and lovingly interact with the growing
population of atheists who think like Dawkins. Being a Christian
means not only being able to give an answer for the hope we have
(1 Peter 3:15), but also pursuing others, so that by God's grace we
may win them for the kingdom (1 Cor. 9:22–23). You do not need
a Ph.D. to dialogue effectively, concisely, and intelligently with an
atheist like Dawkins. This book will increase your knowledge of
atheist thinking and where it is misguided. More importantly, it
will prepare you to use the tools given to us by the Creator to converse with the questioning teenager *and* the college professor. If this
book accomplishes what I hope, by the end you will feel equipped
to humbly and persuasively engage and challenge atheistic belief.

In recent years, atheism has seen a bold and aggressive revival known as the New Atheist movement. The writings of the British biologist and author Richard Dawkins are typical of the arguments and style of this new movement. His rise to prominence is due in no small part to the success of his book *The God Delusion*, published in 2006. The book became a *New York Times* best seller and has sold more than three million copies in more than thirty-five languages.[1]

I saw the popularity of Dawkins's writings firsthand during my early years of graduate school in Boston. Dawkins is a scientist by trade, specializing in evolutionary biology. However, *The God Delusion* clearly made ripples that extended far beyond the ivory towers of scientific elites. I remember sitting on the local Boston subway line, the "T," and observing a variety of people intently reading his book: young men headed into the financial district, silver-haired gentlemen peering through bifocals, and a young mother with a baby in a stroller.

The religious response to Dawkins ran the gamut from outspoken condemnation and retaliation, to detached, indecisive silence, to despairing acceptance. Some Christians who were already nervous about the intersection of science and faith became hypersensitive to any mention of science.

Writers and others in the media produced a flurry of blog posts, editorials, reviews, and responses. The book machine accelerated into overdrive, and, in a few short years, published a small library of responses to Dawkins.[2] Mainstream and social media fueled the controversy, and a number of debates took place. These debates continue with decidedly less frequency, but no less fanfare.[3]

---

1. Richard Dawkins, *Brief Candle in the Dark: My Life in Science* (London: Bantam, 2015), 173.

2. A sampling of these can be found at https://www.catholic.com/magazine/print-edition/dawkins-debunkers.

3. For an example, see the commotion surrounding the debate between Ken Ham and Bill Nye on February 4, 2014.

The secular and scientific communities showered Dawkins with accolades. In 2007, *Time* magazine named him one of the "Top 100 Most Influential People."[4] The *Daily Telegraph* ranked him number 20 in the top 100 living geniuses in 2007.[5] More recently, *Prospect UK* proclaimed Dawkins the top thinker in the world in 2013.[6] It has been more than a decade since the publication of *The God Delusion*, and with the publication of his second memoir in 2015, there is no denying Dawkins's intellectual impact on this world. In light of his impact, it seems appropriate for responsible Christians to reflect on his life, thinking, and contributions.

Despite his renown, there are puzzling inconsistencies. He has begun losing popular support. The same magazine that named him the top thinker in 2013 did not include him at all in 2014.[7] Other atheists are distancing themselves, disavowing his extreme polemics.[8] Dawkins has been disinvited from several speaking engagements[9] as people are increasingly distressed by his sharp, blunt, and frequently indelicate language.[10] Even some

4. http://content.time.com/time/specials/2007/time100/article/0,28804,1595 326_1595329_1616137,00.html.

5. http://www.telegraph.co.uk/news/uknews/1567544/Top-100-living-geniuses .html.

6. http://www.prospectmagazine.co.uk/features/world-thinkers-2013.

7. Jonathan Derbyshire, "Richard Dawkins Was No 1. Now He's off the List of the World's Best Thinkers," *The Guardian*, March 22, 2014. Accessed online at https:// www.theguardian.com/commentisfree/2014/mar/22/goodbye-richard-dawkins -hail-pope-francis-prospect-magazine.

8. Chris Sosa, "I'm Finally Breaking Up with Richard Dawkins," *The Huffington Post*, February 1, 2016. Accessed online at http://www.huffingtonpost.com/chris -sosa/im-finally-breaking-up-with-richard-dawkins_b_9102116.html.

9. See, for example, https://kpfa.org/blog/statement-decision-cancel-richard -dawkins-event/.

10. Sophie Elmhirst, "Is Richard Dawkins Destroying His Reputation?," *The Guardian*, June 9, 2015. Accessed online at https://www.theguardian.com/science /2015/jun/09/is-richard-dawkins-destroying-his-reputation. Adam Lee, "Richard Dawkins has lost it: ignorant sexism gives atheists a bad name," *The Guardian*,

of the most liberal media pundits have condemned his extreme language.[11]

Although the general populace may still conceive of Dawkins as a "great thinker," why have prominent intellectuals been abandoning him recently? Why is there so much variation in how people view him and his ideas? Does he deserve the "great thinker" moniker? How does one define "greatness" in thinking or in anything else? Is it just a popularity contest?

What is actually new about Dawkins and his philosophy? What is the same? How has Dawkins contributed to the way we think today? Is it even fair to try to make these assessments at this juncture in time?

The editors and I asked these questions as we struggled to decide whether Dawkins should receive inclusion in the Great Thinkers series. In the end, although the quality, vigor, and depth of Dawkins's thinking may not qualify as "great," his work has undoubtedly left an indelible mark on popular sentiment. The powerful force of his thinking lies partially in presentation, packaging, and passionate appeal.

A significant number of the existing Christian responses to Dawkins seek to address the specifics of his arguments. Although those responses are necessary and enlightening, there is little discussion of how to talk about Dawkins with others. Where do we go from here? How do we engage with those of his particular strain of belief? As more and more people are adopting atheistic or antireligious views founded on Dawkinsian rhetoric, how can we positively interact with them? I believe our shared creation as

September 18, 2014. Accessed online https://www.theguardian.com/comment isfree/2014/sep/18/richard-dawkins-sexist-atheists-bad-name.

11. Mary Elizabeth Williams, "Stop Pouting, Richard Dawkins: Sharing a Rape 'Joke' Targeting an Activist Is a 'De-platforming' Offense," *Salon*, January 28, 2016. Accessed online at http://www.salon.com/2016/01/28/stop_pouting_richard _dawkins_sharing_a_rape_joke_targeting_an_activist_is_a_de_platforming_ offense/.

humans and the truth revealed in Scripture and nature provide the necessary points of contact for productive dialogue.

In what follows, I aim to provide a palatable, clear, and simple presentation of Dawkins that is accessible, yet thorough and informed. By the end, the reader should be able to understand the relevant issues and feel confident to approach and engage Dawkinsian thinking wherever it is encountered.

1

DAWKINS REVEALED

To learn the specifics of Dawkins's colorful life, you can read his weighty and detailed memoirs. He chronicles his early years in his first memoir, *An Appetite for Wonder* (2013). His second memoir, *Brief Candle in the Dark* (2015), focuses on the later years, including his books and public influence.

Clinton Richard Dawkins was born in Kenya in 1941. Although he was raised with a sense of religious duty by Anglican parents,[1] he claims to have emphatically rejected religion fairly early, due to discomfort with doctrines like original sin and supernatural claims.[2] For Dawkins, learning about Darwin's theory of evolution by natural selection hammered the final nail in God's coffin.[3]

Dawkins studied at Balliol College (Oxford, UK) and

---

1. Richard Dawkins, *An Appetite for Wonder: The Making of a Scientist* (London: Bantam, 2013), 103.

2. Ibid., 139–40.

3. Comments from his debate with John Lennox at the University of Alabama on October 3, 2007.

received a doctoral degree from Oxford University in 1966.[4] He researched ethology (animal behavior) and evolutionary biology under Nobel Prize winner Niko Tinbergen. He focused on ways to mathematically model the pecking decisions of chickens.[5] After a brief stint of teaching at the University of California–Berkeley, he returned to Oxford as a lecturer in zoology, a position he held for twenty years.

During his time as a professor at Oxford, he published his first book, *The Selfish Gene* (1976). In that book, he posits that evolution is not driven by what is best for a group of organisms, but rather by what is best for individual genes. He argues that "we, and all other animals, are machines created by our genes."[6] A scientific reader may see the direct correlation between this reasoning and Dawkins's study of chicken pecking. The thinking goes something like this: "If we can program a computer to accurately predict a chicken's behavior, then what is the difference between a chicken and a complex computer? By extension, what is the difference between a human and a very complex computer? Therefore, humans are nothing more than gene machines, doing what they need to survive." Although we may not agree with this extrapolation and the assumptions contained within it, we can at least develop a plausible understanding of where these ideas came from.

The Selfish Gene changed the way people thought about evolution, and Dawkins has since capitalized a great deal on the success and renown of that book. It still impacts biology more than forty years later,[7] even being voted recently as more inspiring

---

4. Dawkins's CV, available online at http://www.fontem.com/archivos/usuarios/cv_521.pdf.

5. Richard Dawkins, "The Ontogeny of a Pecking Preference in Domestic Chicks," *Zeitschrift für Tierpsychologie* 25 (1968): 170–86.

6. Richard Dawkins, *The Selfish Gene* (Oxford: Oxford University Press, 1976), 2.

7. https://www.edge.org/documents/archive/edge178.html.

than Darwin's *Origin of Species*.[8] Dawkins followed with roughly one book every four years, expanding on the ideas in *The Selfish Gene*. What began as an effort to solidify evolutionary biology gradually morphed into an anti-theist ideology. Dawkins argues that if evolution is true, then certain consequences naturally follow. Not only is a Creator unnecessary for ultimate explanations, but evolution actually provides evidence *against* a personal God. He argues in *The Blind Watchmaker* (1986) that "evolution reveals a universe without design."[9]

In the volumes that followed *The Blind Watchmaker*, Dawkins vehemently contends that evolution "solves" religious questions that were unanswerable until now. For example, he is convinced that the beauty he sees and the wonder he feels in the world are more magnificently attributable to natural causes than to a personal God. *Unweaving the Rainbow* (1998) is an ode to this very sentiment.

The slow march from atheism toward anti-theism reached its culmination in 2006 with the printing of Dawkins's *The God Delusion* and the dawn of the New Atheist movement. *The God Delusion* was published at about the same time as several other anti-theist books by other authors:

- *The End of Faith: Religion, Terror, and the Future of Reason,* by Sam Harris (2004)
- *Atheist Manifesto: The Case against Christianity, Judaism, and Islam,* by Michel Onfray (2005)
- *Breaking the Spell: Religion as a Natural Phenomenon,* by Daniel Dennett (2006)
- *God Is Not Great: How Religion Poisons Everything,* by Christopher Hitchens (2007)

---

8. https://royalsociety.org/news/2017/07/science-book-prize-poll-results/.
9. Richard Dawkins, *The Blind Watchmaker* (New York: W. W. Norton, 1986).

- *God: The Failed Hypothesis—How Science Shows That God Does Not Exist*, by Victor Stenger (2007)

Since then, Dawkins has spent a good deal of his time campaigning for his reasoning in *The God Delusion*, including speaking tours, interviews, and public debates. New Atheism landed cover stories in *Time* magazine[10] and *Wired*.[11] At this point, the reader may want to pause and ask: "We know that atheism has been around for a long time, so what is really new about New Atheism? And what has made it so attractive now?" I will try to address the first question here, and tackle the second question in the next chapter.

At its core, there may not be anything new about New Atheism. One critic contends that, while Dawkins's "book is written with rhetorical passion and power, the stridency of its assertions merely masks tired, weak and recycled arguments."[12] So why the "New" moniker? One possibility is that the title "New Atheism" helps fix it as a particular movement at a particular time in history. However, I believe there is more to it than that.

There are at least three new aspects of New Atheism. First, Dawkins has been mostly a popularizer, gaining at least temporary cultural sway by influencing the masses. He does this by being clear, concise, and simple—to the point of being simplistic. He has not restricted himself to technical treatises for niche communities. He has been active with op-ed articles, Twitter,[13] and a number of other popular forums, employing wit, sarcasm, and withering criticism to draw a clear line in the sand. He understands

10. November 13, 2006: http://content.time.com/time/covers/0,16641,2006
1113,00.html.

11. November 1, 2006: http://archive.wired.com/wired/archive/14.11/.

12. Alister E. McGrath and Joanna Collicutt McGrath, *The Dawkins Delusion?*
(Downers Grove, IL: InterVarsity Press, 2007), 12.

13. Dawkins has more than 2.5 million followers on Twitter: https://twitter.com
/RichardDawkins.

the importance of imagery, analogy, storytelling, and linguistic clarity. These all appeal to the public consciousness and imagination. Followers are not always won by making the best argument, but by making the argument in the best way. Throughout history, the people who have amassed devoted adherents have been those with charisma, passion, zeal, and vision. Dawkins and the New Atheists have a story to tell, and even though their story may be flawed, it paints a convenient and alluring picture.

Second, Dawkins uses new tools to support old arguments, including a mass of new data from biology that substantiates, he believes, a purely evolutionary story of life. The last few decades have brought tremendous advances in our understanding of genetics and of molecular and cell biology. Dawkins, in particular, with his training as a biologist, seeks to interpret this data to his advantage through storytelling. Later, we shall examine whether this storytelling is complete and coherent, or if Dawkins selectively ignores and distorts evidence to fit a preconceived mold.

Finally, Dawkins is "new" in his tone and goals. He is novel "in the intensity of [his] ridicule of religion, not the substance of [his] criticism."[14] His followers are stridently evangelistic. Dawkins says in his preface, "If this book works as I intend, religious readers who open it will be atheists when they put it down."[15] Dawkins has an almost sweeping intolerance of religious tolerance,[16] including agnostic positions. "Dawkins does not merely disagree with religious myths. He disagrees with tolerating them."[17] The unambiguous goal is the abolition of religion from the planet.

14. Alister McGrath, *Why God Won't Go Away* (Nashville: Thomas Nelson, 2010), 43.

15. Richard Dawkins, *The God Delusion* (New York: Houghton Mifflin, 2006, 2008), 28.

16. John F. Haught, *God and the New Atheism* (Louisville: Westminster John Knox, 2008), 10, 37.

17. Gary Wolf, "The Church of the Non-Believers," *Wired*, November 2006. Accessed online at https://www.wired.com/2006/11/atheism/.

During a symposium in La Jolla, California, in November 2006, physicist Steven Weinberg said, "Anything that we scientists can do to weaken the hold of religion should be done, and may in fact be our greatest contribution to civilization."[18] Dawkins pursues this goal, writing with a passion, zeal, and certainty that would be labeled proselytizing if it came from any other religious tradition.

So after all the podium preaching, letter writing, tweeting, arguing, blogging, and publishing, where do we stand more than a decade after this resurgence of atheism?

In many respects, nothing has changed. There are still atheists, and there are still Christians. Scientists still wrestle with the intersection of science and religion. Questions remain unanswered. There is no majority consensus. Secular biologists possess no testable scenarios for the origin of life;[19] secular physicists possess no testable scenarios for the origin of a complex universe; and secular philosophers possess no explanation for the origin of complexity itself.

Yet the landscape has altered in some ways. The militant crusade against religion has relaxed somewhat when met with public resistance and the growing realization that its claims don't reflect reality. Opposition from within the ranks of atheists has contributed to a more tolerant stance. Passion and eloquence may initially stir up zealous followers, but in order to sustain the movement, Dawkins has found it necessary to court favor using opinions more in line with public sentiment.

The seeds of discontent were visible in 2006 during the initial burst onto the scene. At the California symposium mentioned above, attendees agreed that science was losing out to religious

18. Statements at the Science Network's symposium "Beyond Belief: Science, Religion, Reason, and Survival," La Jolla, CA, November 5, 2006.

19. Leroy Cronin and Sara Walker, "Beyond Prebiotic Chemistry," *Science* 352, no. 6290 (June 3, 2016): 1174–75. Accessed online at http://science.sciencemag.org/content/352/6290/1174.full.

belief and debated what strategy should be adopted to rectify the situation. Hardliners like Dawkins wanted to go after religion, guns blazing, but others pointed out that such methods might be offensive and ineffective.[20] The blunt, antagonistic vernacular of Dawkins has actually driven some away from atheism to Christianity.[21] Even atheist philosophers like Michael Ruse take exception to much of what Dawkins has done: "Richard Dawkins in *The God Delusion* would fail any introductory philosophy or religion course. Proudly he criticizes that whereof he knows nothing. . . . *The God Delusion* makes me ashamed to be an atheist."[22] Clearly, Dawkins does not speak for all atheists.

This brings us to the latest developments: Dawkins's publication of two memoirs, totaling roughly 750 pages, in the space of about a year. What is the unspoken goal of these memoirs appearing at this point in time? As noted previously, Dawkins's reputation has recently been declining. His public has become less tolerant of his religious intolerance. Dawkins's marginalization increases as he seeks to be consistent and truthful with his atheism and its unpleasant implications. He must choose either to be truthful and disliked or, by compromising, to be influential and well-liked in the court of public opinion. Dawkins may need to pander to the changing cultural mandates more than he would like to admit, since popularity is tantamount to influence and legacy. His memoirs may be an attempt to help solve this public

20. George Johnson, "A Free-for-All on Science and Religion," *New York Times*, November 21, 2006. Accessed online at http://www.nytimes.com/2006/11/21 /science/21belief.html?_r=1.

21. Eryn Sun, "Former Dawkins Atheist Richard Morgan Continues to Praise God," *The Christian Post*, March 24, 2011. Accessed online at http://www.christian post.com/news/former-dawkins-atheist-richard-morgan-continues-to-praise-god -49558/ and https://www.christiantoday.com/article/richard.dawkins.response.to .suggestions.he.may.actually.be.converting.people.to.christ.oh.dear/36844.htm.

22. http://www.beliefnet.com/columnists/scienceandthesacred/2009/08/why -i-think-the-new-atheists-are-a-bloody-disaster.html.

identity crisis. By describing himself in his own words, Dawkins can paint the softened picture he wants everyone to see.

Unfortunately, the memoirs read like the chronicles of a man trying to pat himself on the back for a job well done and convince himself and the world that he is a decent guy. He gives himself the title of a "natural collaborator"[23] and describes himself as humorous, friendly,[24] compassionate, sensitive, and kind.[25] He frequently name-drops and praises those he has worked with. It sounds more like an acceptance speech for winning a lifetime achievement award from an elitist club than a personal, introspective memoir.

The last half of Dawkins's second memoir is a defense of his books and ideas and a response to critics. In a cultured, gentlemanly tone, he tries to "patch up" public relations issues[26] and explain his sometimes aggressive demeanor in public debates[27] and writing: "I like to think it's a humorous and humane book, far from the angry and strident polemic that is sometimes alleged. Some of the humour is satire, even ridicule, and it's true that the targets of such humour often have a hard time distinguishing good-natured ridicule from hate speech."[28] His self-defense ends up looking more like rationalization than genuine humility.

Therein lies one of the startling omissions of his books: Dawkins does no wrong. At a time when he feels pressured to defend his legacy, he fails to admit to serious mistakes. He cannot accommodate any blunders that may mar his carefully crafted image. He avoids discussion of any real weakness or shortcoming. For example, as a man who has been married three times,

23. Richard Dawkins, *Brief Candle in the Dark: My Life in Science* (London: Bantam, 2015), 64.
24. Ibid., 160.
25. Ibid., 169.
26. Ibid., 212–16.
27. Ibid., 255–62.
28. Ibid., 421.

there is a glaring omission of information about the first two unions. Additionally, he seems to completely ignore debates or encounters that did not end entirely favorably for him.[29]

Though this may seem nonessential, familiarizing ourselves with how Dawkins thinks of himself and how he presents himself *is* essential as we seek to interact with Dawkins and atheists like him. I believe there is a pattern of inconsistency and compromise among atheists. In fact, these traits are necessary hallmarks of their lives and beliefs. Why? Because being fully consistent, committed, and unwavering in godlessness ultimately leads to irrationality, chaos, and despair. Atheists do not *appear* to be hopeless because their actions reveal functional beliefs that are actually inconsistent with their confessed beliefs. This is reflected not only in their stated philosophy, logic, and argumentation, but in the way they live their lives, remaking beliefs and attitudes to make them more palatable to ever-changing public preferences. We will see this as we examine Dawkins's beliefs in more detail in later chapters.

29. A transcript of his 2007 debate with John Lennox can be found at http://www.protorah.com/god-delusion-debate-dawkins-lennox-transcript/.

2

ATHEISM'S ATTRACTIVENESS: WHY SO MUCH APPEAL?

The atheism of Dawkins is a popular, trendy topic. In order for a book on the subject to sell three million copies, it must possess some appeal, something that people gravitate toward. I have included below a short list of some factors that I believe are driving atheism in today's intellectual market. Every individual is unique, so these by no means represent the complete picture. However, they may provide some insights for those seeking to engage Dawkinsian belief.

Appeal to Free Inquiry and Open-Mindedness

At least on the surface, Dawkins appears to be driven by an objective search for the truth. He claims to be unbiased as he weighs evidence and draws conclusions. Dawkins says his goal is an "honest and systematic endeavor to find out the truth about the real world."[1] Another atheist, Christopher Hitchens, puts it

1. Richard Dawkins, *The God Delusion* (New York: Houghton Mifflin, 2006, 2008), 405.

this way: ["What we respect is free inquiry, open-mindedness, and the pursuit of ideas for their own sake. We do not hold our convictions dogmatically."[2] Dawkins professes to use only reason and facts to reach the truth.]

We all want to know the truth, or at least we claim to. Most people recognize that truth is attainable and that the world is rational. And all at least claim to want to know the truth. But how often do we find ourselves seeking evidence to support what we have already decided is true? How willing are we to change our minds?

[Dawkins claims he would abandon evolution and atheism if there were any evidence to disprove them.[3] However, what constitutes sufficient evidence is a matter of no small debate. This also raises the issue of interpretation—whose interpretation of the evidence is the right one? Who decides what the evidence "concludes"? People decide, but all people come with preconceptions and personal agendas. What happens when two people draw different conclusions from the same evidence?

[If we want truth, and we want it to be objective and unbiased,] who or what can provide such assurances? Is science the answer?

Rejecting Atheism Means Rejecting Science, Which Means a Return to the Dark Ages

We have benefited immensely from scientific discoveries. Scientific advances in medicine prolong life, cure disease, and prevent epidemics. Biotechnology and computing make our lives easier through automation, miniaturization, and customization. We have much to be thankful for! Using observation and experimentation, we have been able to overturn faulty beliefs about

2. Christopher Hitchens, *God Is Not Great: How Religion Poisons Everything* (New York: Twelve Books, 2007), 5.

3. Dawkins, *The God Delusion*, 320.

the way the planets move, how heredity works, and what really happens inside a cell.

Although it's not perfect, experimental science remains one of the best systems for ascertaining and pursuing the truth. It is for good reason that people have a high opinion of science. Any insinuation that rejecting atheism would mean halting scientific progress would understandably cause a great deal of consternation. Dawkins has managed to entangle atheism so thoroughly with science that there is no room for any other conclusion. For him, the two are one. You cannot reject the one without abandoning the other.

For Dawkins, believing in God means giving up on the pursuit of science. He puts it this way:

> To suggest that the first cause, the great unknown which is responsible for something existing rather than nothing, is a being capable of designing the universe and of talking to a million people simultaneously, is a total abdication of the responsibility to find an explanation.[4] . . . A lot more work needs to be done, of course, and I'm sure it will be. Such work would never be done if scientists were satisfied with a lazy default such as "intelligent design theory" would encourage. Here is the message that an imaginary "intelligent design theorist" might broadcast to scientists: "If you don't understand how something works, never mind: just give up and say God did it. You don't know how the nerve impulse works? Good! You don't understand how memories are laid down in the brain? Excellent! Is photosynthesis a bafflingly complex process? Wonderful! Please don't go to work on the problem, just give up, and appeal to God."[5]

4. Ibid., 185.
5. Ibid., 159.

Ironically, such an intelligent design theorist would have to be, as Dawkins says, "imaginary," because actual intelligent design scientists pursue science to understand what is currently inexplicable and do not simply "give up."

Dawkins believes that scientific and technological advances are dependent on our adherence to a naturalistic worldview. If we let religion "in," science will stop, and we will lose everything.[6] As retired law professor Phillip Johnson puts it, "Representatives of the scientific establishment have taught us . . . to believe that the success of science in providing technology is tied to the worldview of naturalism, so that any questioning of the worldview endangers the continuance of the technology."[7] Johnson summarizes this erroneous view: "Christianity destroyed classical civilization and brought on a Dark Age. Civilization escaped the Dark Ages only with the rise of the Renaissance man and science. Secular thinking helped shake off the shackles of religion and created the modern world. Today only the vestiges of organized religion prevent humankind from achieving its full potential."[8] Contrary to what Dawkins would lead us to believe, however, the rise of modern science actually owes a great deal to Christian faith.[9]

6. Dawkins has it backwards. Christian faith *encourages* scientific exploration. As Thomas Torrance put it, referring to Francis Bacon, the father of the Scientific Method, "Far from leading to a neglect of nature, the distinction between Grace and nature directed Bacon to the pursuit of natural science as a religious duty, for he understood it to mean that God has kept the Godward side of nature hidden, that is, He has kept final causes or the ultimate law of nature 'within His own curtain,' but whatever is not-God is laid open by God for man's investigation and comprehension." Thomas Torrance, *Theological Science* (Edinburgh, UK: T&T Clark, 1996), 69.

7. Phillip E. Johnson and John Mark Reynolds, *Against All Gods: What's Right and Wrong about the New Atheism* (Downers Grove, IL: InterVarsity Press, 2010), 24.

8. Ibid., 102.

9. See Alfred North Whitehead, *Science and the Modern World* (1925; New York: Free Press, 1997); Nancy Pearcey and Charles Thaxton, *The Soul of Science: Christian Faith and Natural Philosophy* (Wheaton, IL: Crossway, 1994).

People Want to Believe They Are Smart

No one wants to be perceived as unintelligent. So when we are told to make the wise decision or smart choice, we want to be thought of as competent, capable, and bright. Dawkins insults people's intelligence if they are not atheists. In his eyes, intelligence and atheism go hand in hand. You cannot have one without the other. Dawkins himself says, "I suspect that for many people the main reason they cling to religion is . . . that they have been let down by our educational system."[10] He later references several studies to support his claim, saying, "Religiosity is indeed negatively correlated with education (more highly educated people are less likely to be religious). Religiosity is also negatively correlated with interest in science."[11] His message is clear: if you are smart, you are an atheist. "It is absolutely safe to say that if you meet somebody who claims not to believe in evolution, that person is ignorant, stupid or insane (or wicked, but I'd rather not consider that)."[12]

What if two people see the same facts and arrive at different conclusions? According to Dawkins, you are only smart if you agree with him. Of course, he provides no evidence for his implication that intelligence correlates with correctness all the time. Very smart people can make very wrong statements.

Atheism and Evolution Provide
Simple, Clear Narratives

Atheists tell a great story. They publish impressive diagrams showing the gradual morphing of species to species. One

10. Dawkins, *The God Delusion*, 22.
11. Ibid., 129.
12. Richard Dawkins, "Richard Dawkins Review of Blueprints: Solving the Mystery of Evolution," *New York Times*, April 9, 1989, section 7. Accessed online at http://www.philvaz.com/apologetics/p88.htm.

description of a debate tells it this way: "Hitchens told the better, more coherent story. He did not have much evidence for this tale and could not defend it in detail, but he told it well and it was attractive due to its extreme simplicity."[13] Although the literature is replete with such tales, we will address two of them here.

> One side of the mountain is a sheer cliff, impossible to climb, but on the other side is a gentle slope to the summit. On the summit sits a complex device such as an eye or a bacterial flagellar motor. The absurd notion that such complexity could spontaneously self-assemble is symbolized by leaping from the foot of the cliff to the top in one bound. Evolution, by contrast, goes around the back of the mountain and creeps up the gentle slope to the summit: easy! The principle of climbing the gentle slope as opposed to leaping up the precipice is so simple, one is tempted to marvel that it took so long for a Darwin to arrive on the scene and discover it.[14]

Or, to be more specific:

> Here's how some scientists think some eyes may have evolved: The simple light-sensitive spot on the skin of some ancestral creature gave it some tiny survival advantage, perhaps allowing it to evade a predator. Random changes then created a depression in the light-sensitive patch, a deepening pit that made "vision" a little sharper. At the same time, the pit's opening gradually narrowed, so light entered through a small aperture, like a pinhole camera.
>
> Every change had to confer a survival advantage, no matter how slight. Eventually, the light-sensitive spot evolved into a

13. Johnson and Reynolds, *Against All Gods*, 103.
14. Dawkins, *The God Delusion*, 147.

retina, the layer of cells and pigment at the back of the human eye. Over time a lens formed at the front of the eye. It could have arisen as a double-layered transparent tissue containing increasing amounts of liquid that gave it the convex curvature of the human eye.[15]

These stories grip the imagination, but unfortunately, science is not about pulling "plausible scenarios" out of a hat and telling a Kipling "just-so" story. We have to do more than imagine.[16] Herein lies Dawkins's primary blind spot—the simplicity belies a weakness. Stories can deceptively hide or ignore complications or inconvenient truths.[17] For example, anyone can imagine a "gentle slope" to the top, but what if no such slope of evolution exists in reality? In fact, no "gentle slope" has ever been demonstrated. It is akin to saying that because we can imagine that the pickup truck was invented when a really big rock fell on the back of an SUV and made a truck bed, it must be so. This story misses many of the complex changes and intelligent engineering necessary for truck construction. Imagination and story do not constitute concrete evidence and do not imply plausibility.[18]

15. PBS Library. Accessed online at http://www.pbs.org/wgbh/evolution/library/01/1/l_011_01.html. For a more technical attempt, see T. D. Lamb, S. P. Collin, and E. N. Pugh Jr., "Evolution of the Vertebrate Eye: Opsins, Photoreceptors, Retina, and Eye Cup," *Nature Reviews Neuroscience* 8, no. 12 (December 8, 2007): 960–76. Accessed online at https://www.ncbi.nlm.nih.gov/pmc/articles/PMC3143066/. See another such story about the eye in Richard Dawkins, *Climbing Mount Improbable* (New York: W. W. Norton, 1996), 126–79.

16. Yet, even leading biology textbooks resort to this kind of fantastical language when dealing with origins stories: "propose," "speculative," "may have been," "possible," "might have," "evidently," "hypothetical scheme," "presumably," "suggest," "mystery," "plausible view." From Lisa A. Urry, Michael L. Cain, et al., *Campbell Biology in Focus*, 2nd ed. (New York: Pearson, 2015), and Bruce Alberts, Alexander D. Johnson, et al., *Molecular Biology of the Cell*, 6th ed. (New York: Garland Science, 2014).

17. A geocentric solar system with circular orbits for the planets was a simple and clear story, but ended up being incorrect.

18. For more on how we must differentiate between "lovely" stories and "likely"

Atheism Brings Freedom

Tied in with the notion of simplicity is the idea of freedom. It has been suggested, and current polling data could support the conclusion, that people are more interested in believing that God does not exist than they are in saying that they believe in atheism.[19] It is easier to say no than to say yes and commit yourself. Being "nonreligious" fits well with the current cultural trends of pluralism and indecision.

Religion is portrayed as confining, controlling, and restricting, while atheism appears freeing.[20] On the surface, this seems to be true. If there is no God, then I am not responsible to anyone or anything. I can define life on my own terms. There is no ultimate judgment by, or accountability to, anyone.[21] Each man becomes a law unto himself. "In those days there was no king in Israel. Everyone did what was right in his own eyes" (Judg. 21:25). We are enticed by the idea of autonomy, realized in self-definition and self-fulfillment. In reality, these are illusions, since we are all constrained by what we serve (2 Peter 2:19). We cannot live a life committed to nothing. We just want to avoid vocalizing those commitments, thereby pretending to be completely autonomous.

For the time being, let us simply say that atheism brings its own set of worries and constraints, and that many Christian believers, myself included, have found true freedom in Christianity (Matt. 11:29–30; John 8:32; Rom. 8:2). "God's moral order is designed by God to guide us into personal fellowship and satisfaction. It

---

stories, see Peter Lipton, "Inference to the Best Explanation," in *A Companion to the Philosophy of Science*, W. H. Newton-Smith, ed. (Malden, MA: Blackwell Publishing, 2000), 184–93.

19. John Lennox, *Gunning for God: Why the New Atheists Are Missing the Target* (Oxford: Lion Hudson, 2011), 19.

20. Elaine Howard Ecklund, *Science vs. Religion: What Scientists Really Think* (Oxford: Oxford University Press, 2010), 55.

21. Morality is discussed more fully in chapter 11.

is for our good. It is for our freedom, we might say, in the true sense of 'freedom.' The person who goes astray from God's wise guidance burdens himself with sorrows and frustrations.[22] If you view God as dictatorial, tyrannical, and malevolent, I can understand why atheism would be attractive, but this is not the Christian God. From the Christian perspective, this makes sense in another way, too. Without God, man becomes God, and man has always wanted to be God. This is the fundamental idolatry in humanity.

We resist the idea of submitting to an authority because we have mostly experienced broken, sinful systems imposed by flawed humans, not the love of a perfect God. The atheistic story of perceived freedom matches what our sinful hearts have been drawn to since the fall of Adam: a narrative that appeals to our rebellion against God. In addition, perceived misdirection, inaction, or wrongful direction from God leads people to reject him because he does not line up with their conception of what love should look like. In this case, they are free to construct a god (or non-god) of their own liking, who serves their interests. Dawkins and people like him are quick to forget their own limitations and human finitude and reject God because they, as creatures, cannot fathom the infinite depth and eternal plan of the Creator (Isa. 55:8–9; Rom. 9:20).

Atheism Promises to Rid the World of Evil

This world we are in is not right. Racism, violence, deceit, injustice—the list goes on. We all see it or experience it in different ways. What is so wrong with the world? Dawkins claims to have found a cause for these problems: faith! Why is there

22. Vern Poythress, *Inerrancy and Worldview: Answering Modern Challenges to the Bible* (Wheaton IL: Crossway, 2012), 24.

so much suffering? <u>Faith</u>! What is the answer? Get <u>rid of faith.</u>
<u>Eradicate religion.</u>

Dawkins presents a beautiful scenario in his preface:

> Imagine no suicide bombers, no 9/11, no 7/7, no Crusades,
> no witch-hunts, no Gunpowder Plot, no Indian partition, no
> Israeli/Palestinian wars, no Serb/Croat/Muslim massacres,
> no persecution of Jews as "Christ-killers," no Northern Ireland
> "troubles," no "honour killings," no shiny-suited bouffant-haired
> televangelists fleecing gullible people of their money. . . . Imag-
> ine no Taliban to blow up ancient statues, no public behead-
> ings of blasphemers, no flogging of female skin for the crime of
> showing an inch of it.[23]

That sounds marvelous! I also long to live in a world where
atrocities like those never happen. Of course, Dawkins's misguided conclusion is that religion is the common denominator.
He should consider that maybe it is the people themselves that
are the issue, and that the varying claims of allegiance to religions
are rationalizations for preexisting heart attitudes. And Dawkins
conveniently forgets much of the good done by Christians (Matt.
5:44) and the litany of horrors perpetrated by antireligious
groups, including communist Russia and China.

Lennox summarizes Dawkins's omission nicely:

> I would like to ask you also to imagine a world with no atheism.
> No Stalin, no Mao, no Pol Pot, just to name the heads of the
> three officially atheistic states that were responsible for some
> of the worst mass crimes of the twentieth century. Just imag-
> ine a world with no Gulag, no Cultural Revolution, no Killing
> Fields, no removal of children from their parents because the

23. Dawkins, *The God Delusion*, 23–24.

parents were teaching them about their beliefs, no refusal of higher education to believers in God, no discrimination against believers in the workplace, no pillaging, destruction and burning of places of worship.[24]

Christians would argue that sin is present in the hearts of all humans (Rom. 3:23), but no one wants to consider that he may be part of the problem. It is much easier to blame someone or something else. So, by targeting religion instead of people, individuals can rest easy and not have to deal with the difficult task of looking inward at their own behavior and motivations. Religion provides a convenient, culturally acceptable scapegoat.

The circumstances of September 11, 2001, changed the tenor of the Western world. Religious extremism has touched us all, becoming a legitimate fear. The New Atheists have cashed in on the fear that swept America in the wake of those terrorist acts. Religious extremism is hard to define, hone in on, and eradicate. It is easy to see its results, but much harder to identify the roots and catch it in its infancy. Dawkins has taken the simplest, albeit the most extreme, position: lump religious extremism in with all religious thought. But doing so avoids careful deliberation and discussion and incriminates people before they even commit a crime. Saying that all religion is bad is like trying to eliminate obesity by outlawing food, thus throwing out the baby with the bathwater.

Atheists want to get rid of evil—an admirable goal. If they think religion is the problem, they should be able to point to some community, country, or system in the history of the world that is religion-free and devoid of evil. They need to prove that evil is not simply a common denominator of human existence in a fallen world.

24. Lennox, *Gunning for God*, 83.

The Heart of the Matter

As Christians seeking to engage our atheist family members, friends, and neighbors, we need to understand what drives them at their core. This is not a war of information or a pure conflict of ideas. It is a battle for the heart. Satan will use whatever means he can to capture a person's heart (1 Peter 5:8). Ultimately, people believe atheism partly because they believe it is factually true, but also because they believe it fills some need or desire in their hearts. Whether that is the desire for self-rule and autonomy, the desire for knowledge, or the desire to be free from fear, the heart is always in play. Understanding Dawkins's appeal will help you understand the real live person in front of you.

Atheist Michael Shermer, founder of the Skeptics Society, points out that "people seem to double down on their beliefs in the teeth of overwhelming evidence against them. . . . [They may even] spin-doctor facts to fit preconceived beliefs to reduce dissonance. . . . Why? Because it threatens their worldview."[25] We want a belief system that allows us to justify what we have already decided in our hearts. Aldous Huxley once said, "Those who detect no meaning in the world generally do so because, for one reason or another, it suits their books that the world should be meaningless."[26]

If we are not addressing these underlying heart motivations, no amount of clever argument or clear logic will sway someone. I once heard R. C. Sproul say, "You can win the argument and lose the man." In order to better love and engage our atheist friends, we need to understand them as living, feeling, hurting

25. Michael Shermer, "How to Convince Someone When Facts Fail," *Scientific American*, January 1, 2017. Accessed online at https://www.scientificamerican.com/article/how-to-convince-someone-when-facts-fail/.

26. Aldous Huxley, *Ends and Means: An Inquiry into the Nature of Ideas and into the Methods Employed for Their Realization* (New York: Harper & Brothers, 1937), 273.

humans made in the image of God. Showing the logical failure of atheistic belief may be a necessary step, but our ultimate desire is to express how Christianity fulfills the deepest needs of the heart. God's story is the most appealing of all stories. It is full of human brokenness, wandering, and selfishness, climaxes with a grand rescue by the hero, and results in our living happily ever after, spending an eternity with our perfect Creator. This amazing story is not only captivating, but true. In Christ we have real freedom, purpose, love, and hope, and this is a truth we desire our atheist friends (including Dawkins) to rationally and wholeheartedly embrace.

3

CURRENT INFLUENCE

It is important to understand that the brand of atheism that springs from Dawkins's beliefs is not indifferent and inactive. Though there is no need to be alarmist, consequences necessarily flow from any philosophical perspective. These things have tangible influences in our world.

Atheism is not an absence of belief. It is belief in an absence. It has ramifications for existence and how you live your life. We have to be careful not to make the same mistake that Dawkins makes about theists: just because a person claims to be an atheist, that does not mean that his actions flow directly from atheist dogma or are to be blamed or pinned on atheism. So, what can we say about atheism and its implications?

David Brooks, a writer for the *New York Times*, points out that atheism and the Darwinist foundation on which it rests have wide-ranging effects: "Scarcely a month goes by when *Time* or *Newsweek* doesn't have a cover article on how our genes shape everything from our exercise habits to our mood. Science sections are filled with articles on how brain structure influences things like lust and learning . . . while evolutionary theory reshapes psychology, dieting, and literary criticism. Confident and exhilarated, evolutionary theorists believe they have a universal framework to explain human behavior."[1] If humans can be explained, they can be predicted, shaped, changed, and controlled. There is an almost inbuilt prerogative to manipulate.[2]

Dawkins's perspective cannot be isolated and separated from common life. By definition, as a worldview, it affects everything and cannot be confined to the realm of science alone. A worldview, if correct, is like a restorative elixir that slowly works throughout the whole body: cleaning, renewing, and putting life in order and making it beautiful. However, if wrong, a worldview is like an acid—it eventually eats through, permeates, and destroys everything.[3]

One disconcerting result of Dawkins's atheism is the suggestion that once someone is fully educated, to believe anything besides atheism is insane. Dawkins points out that one of the beauties of science is being able to "publicly explain it to somebody else, not as your opinion or belief but as something that they, when they have understood your reasoning, will feel compelled to accept."[4] This leaves little room for differences of opinion, interpretation, or choice. By contrast, fellow atheist

1. David Brooks, "The Age of Darwin," *New York Times*, April 15, 2007, WK14. Accessed online at http://www.nytimes.com/2007/04/15/opinion/15brooks.html?_r=0.

2. Dawkins himself says, "I wonder whether, some 60 years after Hitler's death, we might at least venture to ask what the moral difference is between breeding for musical ability and forcing a child to take music lessons. Or why it is acceptable to train fast runners and high jumpers but not to breed them." Richard Dawkins, "From the Afterword," *The Herald Scotland*, November 20, 2006. Accessed online at http://www.heraldscotland.com/news/12760676.From_the_Afterword/.

3. For some historical context and commentary, see Richard Weikart, *From Darwin to Hitler: Evolutionary Ethics, Eugenics, and Racism in Germany* (New York: Palgrave Macmillan, 2006), and Richard Weikart, *The Death of Humanity: And the Case for Life* (Washington, DC: Regnery Faith, 2016).

4. Richard Dawkins, *The God Delusion* (New York: Houghton Mifflin, 2006, 2008), 410.

Hitchens has this to say about belief: we have a "right not to believe or be compelled to believe."[5] Hitchens complains that this kind of "thought policing" is only done by religious groups: "All major confrontations over the right to free thought, free speech, and free inquiry have taken the same form—of a religious attempt to assert the literal and limited mind over the ironic and inquiring one."[6] However, this is clearly not the case (e.g., Tiananmen Square).

Dawkins ends up saying, in essence, that we can believe whatever we want, so long as we do not believe anything deemed "dangerous." One result of this is the desire to eliminate religious upbringings. In a televised interview with Jill Mytton, Dawkins said, "You use the words religious abuse. If you were to compare the abuse of bringing up a child really to believe in hell . . . how do you think that would compare in trauma terms with sexual abuse?" She replied, "That's a very difficult question. . . . I think there are a lot of similarities actually, because it is about abuse of trust; it is about denying the child the right to feel free and open and able to relate to the world in the normal way. . . . It's a form of denigration; it's a form of denial of the true self in both cases."[7]

Dawkins follows with a quote from a lecture by Nicholas Humphrey:

> Children, I'll argue, have a human right not to have their minds crippled by exposure to other people's bad ideas—no matter who these other people are. Parents, correspondingly, have no God-given license to enculturate their children in whatever ways they personally choose. . . . In short, children have a right not to have their minds addled by nonsense, and we as a society

5. Christopher Hitchens, *God Is Not Great: How Religion Poisons Everything* (New York: Twelve Books, 2007), 252.

6. Ibid., 258.

7. Dawkins, *The God Delusion*, 365–66.

have a duty to protect them from it. So we should no more allow parents to teach their children to believe, for example, in the literal truth of the Bible or that the planets rule their lives, than we should allow parents to knock their children's teeth out or lock them in a dungeon.[8]

One wonders if Humphrey would think it is abuse to teach kids, as some atheists believe, that there is no ultimate purpose for their life. Dawkins believes, "Faith can be very very dangerous, and deliberately to implant it into the vulnerable mind of an innocent child is a grievous wrong."[9] And yet that is exactly what Dawkins would have us do: implant *his* faith into the minds of school children. Who says it is wrong to pass along what you believe? After all, he is trying to pass along what he believes to us, his readers.

In a moment of humility, Dawkins points out that deciding what is nonsense and what is harmful dogma is a matter of opinion. Science has made mistakes in the past. He instead says that "children should be taught not so much what to think as how to think."[10] Who then teaches them how to think? If atheists can teach evidence from an atheistic perspective, can Christians teach evidence from a Christian perspective? After all, we cannot detach ourselves from our beliefs, even when teaching others how to think.[11] We cannot help but try to impress on our children what we believe, even if it is a philosophy on how to believe.

Finally, ideas have teeth. They do not just sit out there apart from reality. We demonstrate our beliefs in how we behave.

8. Ibid., 366–67. Originally published in Nicholas Humphrey, "What Shall We Tell the Children?," in *The Values of Science: Oxford Amnesty Lectures*, ed. W. Williams (Boulder, CO: Westview, 1998).

9. Dawkins, *The God Delusion*, 348.

10. Ibid., 367.

11. Even science isn't free from the influence of human beliefs. See chapter 6.

For example, we would all agree that sacrificing a one-year-old baby on an altar of fire to the idol Molech is a terrible crime, but what about sacrificing an unborn baby on the altar of personal convenience? The primary reason given for abortions in the US is that the child would be inconvenient, either financially or socially.[12] Christians and atheists think differently about the value of human life and therefore will teach differently about an issue like abortion. We cannot exclude these beliefs from the public forum any more than Dawkins can resist advocating for policies based on his atheist conclusions. How do we deal with this discrepancy? Atheist neuroscientist Sam Harris says, "Some propositions are so dangerous that it may even be ethical to kill people for believing them."[13] Who decides what we are allowed to believe and how those decisions are made? For example, when authoritarian governments (as in communist countries) decide to eliminate "dangerous, divisive, or dissident" speech or beliefs, oppression and terror have been the inevitable results.

Ultimately, Dawkins's ideas will necessarily have downstream effects in day-to-day living—at school, in politics, and at the workplace—and it is therefore incumbent on us to understand, analyze, and critique those ideas.

---

12. William Robert Johnson, "Reasons Given for Having Abortions in the United States," survey by the Alan Guttmacher Institute, 2016. Accessed online at http://www.johnstonsarchive.net/policy/abortion/abreasons.html.

13. Sam Harris, *The End of Faith: Religion, Terror, and the Future of Reason* (New York: W. W. Norton, 2004), 52–53.

4

MAIN TENETS AND BELIEFS

Atheism as Religion

One of the confounding aspects of interacting with Dawkins is the difficulty in pinpointing what he does believe. He vehemently proclaims unbelief in God, but aside from that, there is very little in the way of building a positive case for his own worldview. Most of Dawkins's books are devoted to trying to convince people what not to believe, instead of talking about what to believe. All that being said, Dawkins and the New Atheists do have some shared beliefs. John Lennox describes these core elements well:

> New Atheists are not simply atheists, they are anti-theists. Not believing in God does not leave them in a passive, negative, innocuous vacuum. Their books are replete with all the positive beliefs that flow from their anti-theism. These beliefs form their credo, their faith—much as they like to deny that they have one . . . . Dawkins is surely quoting Julian Baggini, with approval on the meaning of an atheist's commitment to naturalism, when he writes: "What most atheists do *believe*

[italics mine] is that although there is only one kind of stuff in the universe and it is physical, out of this stuff come minds, beauty, emotions, moral values—in short the full gamut of phenomena that gives richness to human life." Just a little later in the text Dawkins says (no longer quoting Baggini or anyone else): "An atheist in this sense of philosophical naturalist is somebody who *believes* [italics mine] there is nothing beyond the natural, physical world, no supernatural creative intelligence lurking behind the observable universe . . ." In light of his own statements, one wonders by what intellectual contortions Dawkins can persuade himself that his atheism is not a *belief* system—his faith shines out too clearly.[1]

This brings us to a very important point in our discussion of Dawkins. It is almost imperative for him that his beliefs remain obscure and ill-defined, because to admit to beliefs sounds a lot like having a religion. Dawkins never defines religion, although he primarily targets Christianity, Judaism, and Islam. But can he categorically exclude atheism? What prevents him from labeling atheism as a religion? Once atheism becomes just another religion, it is subject to the same criticisms that have been leveled against religion.

Undoubtedly, Dawkins would avoid this difficulty by defining religion to exclude atheism. To avoid the appearance of holding to a religion, Dawkins and others are reduced to semantic contortions and indecipherable statements like: "Our belief is not a belief. Our principles are not a faith."[2] And yet, as Chris Hedges, a Pulitzer Prize–winning journalist, points out, "Those who in

1. John Lennox, *Gunning for God: Why the New Atheists Are Missing the Target* (Oxford: Lion Hudson, 2011), 86. He quotes Richard Dawkins, *The God Delusion* (New York: Houghton Mifflin, 2006, 2008), 34.

2. Christopher Hitchens, *God Is Not Great: How Religion Poisons Everything* (New York: Twelve Books, 2007), 5.

the name of science claim that we can overcome our imperfect human nature create a belief system that functions like religion."[3]

Although Dawkins may position atheism to be excluded by a definition of "religion," it appears, functions, and acts like other religions. Atheism provides a worldview: a large-scale meaning for existence. It explains "what matters and why," even if the answers are unpleasant and disheartening.

Atheism is a system of belief that arises naturally and inexorably from the naturalistic worldview, which we will explore in chapter 6. It is impossible to have no beliefs. This has been acknowledged in practice, if not in name, in Britain, where non-religious schools are now required to teach atheism alongside Christianity, Islam, and other religions. "The Religious Studies GCSE 'ensures pupils understand the diversity of religious beliefs in Great Britain' by letting pupils choose the study of both religious and non-religious views."[4]

You may be able to dress up a pig and change its name, but it is still a pig. Simply calling atheism "nonreligious" does not make it so. Can you imagine the uproar if this kind of nomenclature were applied elsewhere? For example, "The mathematics department is now mandated to let pupils choose the study of both mathematical and nonmathematical views." Atheists have even begun assembling in communities that very closely resemble churches: groups of people socializing, listening to a "sermon of sorts," and sharing "thoughts on what they believe."[5] We have more in common than Dawkins realizes.

3. Chris Hedges, *I Don't Believe in Atheists* (New York: Free Press, 2008), 54.

4. Javier Espinoza, "All Pupils at Non-faith Schools Must Study Atheism, Judge Rules," *The Telegraph*, November 25, 2015. Accessed online at http://www.telegraph .co.uk/education/12015859/Non-religious-views-should-not-have-been-left-out -of-new-GCSE-High-Court-rules.html. See also https://www.theguardian.com /education/2015/dec/01/religious-education-atheism-humanism-schools -pupils-gcse.

5. David Zax, "True Nonbeliever," *Yale Alumni Magazine*, July/August 2016, 31–33.

Atheistic Beliefs

Dawkins's brand of religious atheism comes with a devotion to certain beliefs. John Haught, a Catholic professor at Georgetown University, helpfully summarizes these foundational beliefs in his book *God and the New Atheism*:

1. Apart from nature, which includes human beings and our cultural creations, there is nothing. There is no God, no soul, and no life beyond death.
2. Nature is self-originating, not the creation of God.
3. The universe has no overall point or purpose, although individual human lives can be lived purposefully.
4. Since God does not exist, all explanations and all causes are purely natural and can be understood only by science.
5. All the various features of living beings, including human intelligence and behavior, can be explained ultimately in purely natural terms, and today this usually means in evolutionary, specifically Darwinian terms.
6. Faith in God is the cause of innumerable evils and should be rejected on moral grounds.
7. Morality does not require belief in God, and people behave better without faith than with it.[6]

We should note, in passing, that although proposition 3 denies any actual purpose for life, it acknowledges a human desire for purpose. In addition, proposition 6 states that we can make moral judgments. However, this is problematic, since morals and purpose go hand in hand. You cannot have one without the other, since immorality is defined as a violation of purpose.

6. John F. Haught, *God and the New Atheism* (Louisville: Westminster John Knox, 2008), xiii–xiv.

For example, we can say that murder is wrong only if it violates some standard of human purpose, such as "seeking not to harm others." This could present an opportunity in our apologetic style to address a point of "disconnect." Now that we have discussed some of Dawkins's beliefs, we shall investigate how he goes about communicating those beliefs and interacting with competing viewpoints.

5

HOW DAWKINS ARGUES

Interacting with Dawkins, or anyone else who disagrees with you, necessitates understanding how they present their arguments. Perceiving common rhetorical elements and themes can help you make informed decisions about what to respond to and how. Our challenging yet crucial task is to identify these elements, all the while caring and silently praying for the person in front of us. Understanding their rhetorical moves can help us move past confusing verbiage and complicated data to substantive discussion. For example, although Dawkins asks some very good questions that we need to examine thoughtfully and answer humbly, he also employs numerous types of illegitimate argumentation.[1]

---

1. See Norman J. Lund, "Dawkins Debunked: A Dozen Logical Fallacies in *The God Delusion*," available online at http://www.oxfordtutorials.com/Dawkins%20 Debunked%20Summary.htm.

Logical Considerations

Ad Hominem[2]

An ad hominem argument is a statement directed against a specific person instead of against the argument they are espousing. Unsubstantiated name-calling is a good example. For example, Dawkins describes Mother Teresa as a "sanctimonious hypocrite."[3] This accusation fails to address any of the truth claims she has made about God. It merely serves to distract from the logical construction of an argument by trying to impugn the character of the person making an argument.

No True Scotsman Fallacy

This particular fallacy involves reinterpreting or dismissing evidence in order to avoid refutation. Contradictory evidence is declared to be irrelevant simply because it is contradictory. For example, Dawkins says, "Evolution is a fact. . . . No reputable scientist disputes it, and no unbiased reader will close the book doubting it."[4] Actually, a large number of scientists disagree with Darwinism,[5] but by his statement he simply labels them all as disreputable, so that he does not have to take their arguments seriously. In other words, "No one disagrees, and those who do disagree are not worth interacting with."

By Consensus

A subset of the above argument tries to emphasize popular agreement by saying there is a scientific consensus on a particular

---

2. A simple, yet more thorough explanation of various logical fallacies can be found at http://www.logicalfallacies.info/.

3. Richard Dawkins, *The God Delusion* (New York: Houghton Mifflin, 2006, 2008), 330.

4. Richard Dawkins, *The Greatest Show on Earth* (New York: Free Press, 2009), 9.

5. See http://www.dissentfromdarwin.org/.

issue. Remember, however, that at one point there was a scientific consensus on a geocentric solar system. Although it should bring us to careful consideration if many disagree with us, Boaz Miller points out that "the existence of agreement in a community of researchers is a contingent fact, and researchers may reach a consensus for all kinds of reasons, such as fighting a common foe or sharing a common bias. Scientific consensus, by itself, does not necessarily indicate the existence of shared knowledge among the members of the consensus community."[6]

Begging the Question (Circular Reasoning)

This occurs when someone assumes what he is trying to prove. For example, Dawkins declares, "Creative intelligences, being evolved, necessarily arrive late in the universe, and therefore cannot be responsible for designing it."[7] In this example, Dawkins assumes the truth of evolution as an explanation of universe design in order to rule out creative intelligence as an explanation for universe design. Another version of this fallacy states, "God cannot exist because everything that exists must have a natural, material cause." This statement assumes that everything must have a natural, material cause in order to prove that only natural, material things exist. In other words, to prove God's nonexistence, the nonexistence of the supernatural has been assumed.

Academic Considerations

Straw Man Argument

This occurs when someone sets up a false or drastically weakened position and represents it as a real position. In other

6. Boaz Miller, "When Is Consensus Knowledge Based? Distinguishing Shared Knowledge from Mere Agreement," *Synthese* 190, no. 7 (May 2013). Truth is not determined by popularity.

7. Dawkins, *The God Delusion*, 52.

words, someone exaggerates, misrepresents, fabricates, distorts, or otherwise twists an opponent's position in order to refute it. So, in the end, he refutes a position that no one really holds. For example, Dawkins proclaims, "Religious faith is an especially potent silencer of rational calculation . . . because it discourages questioning, by its very nature."[8] But this is not what Christians believe. The Bible says, "Test everything; hold fast what is good" (1 Thess. 5:21).[9] Dawkins proceeds to misrepresent some in the scientific community as well: "[Intelligent Design] leaps straight from the difficulty—'I can't see any solution to the problem'—to the cop-out—'Therefore a Higher Power must have done it.'"[10] Intelligent Design proponents are actually quite careful to disavow this faulty reasoning and strive to make a positive, scientific case for intelligent causation as an inference to the best explanation.[11] In a special case, the straw man misattribution is directed against the God of the Bible, and we will examine a few examples of this in more detail in chapter 8.

In any debate or conflict of ideas, in order to proceed, individuals must be sitting at the same table. In other words, we must agree on the things we are talking about. For example, it does me no good to refute X if my opponent actually believes Y. You should be able to state your opponent's own views in a way they would agree with.[12] This is not only a foundational principle of apologetics; it is also the most loving and considerate way to dialogue with anyone. Any of us can fall prey to the straw man fallacy, but Dawkins makes this mistake repeatedly.

8. Ibid., 346.

9. See also Isa. 1:18; James 3:17

10. Richard Dawkins, "Foreword," in *God, the Devil, and Darwin: A Critique of Intelligent Design Theory,* by Niall Shanks (New York: Oxford University Press, 2004), ix.

11. See William A. Dembski, *The Design Revolution* (Downers Grove, IL: InterVarsity Press, 2004).

12. By God's grace, I seek to do exactly that with atheistic beliefs throughout this book—ideally, to help you make their argument for them, better than they can!

Shoddy Scholarship

Although shoddy scholarship isn't a fallacy as such, it is included here because of its particularly pernicious effects. Often readers can see a logical fallacy, but a lack of pertinent and relevant information can severely skew a reader's conclusions. If Dawkins is going to wade into territory that he is not familiar with, it is honorable and appropriate to acknowledge his limitations or do the requisite research.

Since Dawkins is not an expert in theology, yet his conclusions have theological implications, he attempts to cover himself by quoting an analogy made by P. Z. Myers in reference to the tale of the emperor's new clothes.[13] The basic idea is that you do not need to know theology in order to make a scientific claim about God. Therefore, Dawkins thinks he can simply dismiss the entire field of theology. This claim is tenuous at best, since God's existence would absolutely affect how science is done and how scientific claims are made. Regardless, he voids any defense he might have had when he begins making theological assertions. He cannot justifiably attempt a theological argument for God's nonexistence while ignoring the vast theological literature on the subject.

Dawkins writes blatant untruths about Jesus, Christians, and the Bible. For example, he says, "Jesus limited his in-group of the saved strictly to Jews, in which respect he was following the Old Testament tradition, which was all he knew."[14] And again, "'Love thy neighbour' didn't mean what we now think it means. It meant only 'Love another Jew.'"[15] This flies in the face of what Jesus himself said, as related in the parable of the Good Samaritan (Luke 10:25–37) and the Great Commission (Matt.

---

13. Dawkins, *The God Delusion*, 14–15.
14. Ibid., 288.
15. Ibid., 287.

28:16–20).[16] Dawkins never mentions these passages or offers any explanation.[17]

But what if we decide to give Dawkins the benefit of the doubt? Let us suppose that, even though most Christians do not believe what Dawkins attributes to them, there is someone out there who does. Why does Dawkins choose to engage these misguided forms of Christianity? Why doesn't he engage the top minds, the scholars, the thoughtful, deliberate, and compassionate? Dawkins explains:

> If only such subtle, nuanced religion predominated, the world would surely be a better place, and I would have written a different book. The melancholy truth is that this kind of understated, decent, revisionist religion is numerically negligible. To the vast majority of believers around the world, religion all too closely resembles what you hear from the likes of Robertson, Falwell or Haggard, Osama bin Laden or the Ayatollah Khomeini. These are not straw men, they are all too influential, and everybody in the modern world has to deal with them.[18]

This is perhaps the most remarkable admission in the entire book. It is true that there are harmful theologians and people doing evil under the guise of Christianity; however, Dawkins has just admitted that this is not everyone. Yet he lumps all Christian believers into one category in his book. He makes no distinction between evangelical theologians and "gospel-lite" televangelists. However, he contradicts himself in his own preface by admitting

16. Jesus embodies this in his actions, too, as demonstrated by his healing of the Roman centurion's servant (Matt. 8:5–13).

17. For additional discussion of Dawkins's biblical misinterpretations, see David Marshall, *The Truth behind the New Atheism: Responding to the Emerging Challenges to God and Christianity* (Eugene, OR: Harvest House Publishers, 2007).

18. Dawkins, *The God Delusion*, 15.

that there *are* differences. One wonders how he would feel if we were to group him in with "rabble-rousing" atheists like Stalin. Just because someone misuses the scientific method to unleash a bio-weapon, that does not mean that science is inherently evil.[19] If I want to show that science needs to be displaced, I need to deal with the best of science and the top philosophers and thinkers, not just the popularizers or the worst practitioners. Similarly, just because someone misuses the name of Christ, it does not mean that Christianity is untrue. If Dawkins wants to disprove the existence of God, addressing the proclamations of a few radical individuals is not a compelling or convincing tactic.[20]

Is Dawkins trying to deal with truth or only what happens to be popular? If the latter, then he can ignore serious theologians and philosophers, but he needs to be up-front about this and the limitations of his inferences. His conclusions cannot extend to all of religion, and certainly not to traditional Christianity. If Dawkins pursues truth, then the academically responsible method is to engage the toughest and most thoughtful forms of religion. He cannot pretend that the loudest voices speak for everyone or that lasting influence is correlated with volume. This is equivalent to me dissecting a famous actor's views on economic policy and making sweeping conclusions about our nation, while neglecting experts at the Federal Reserve, on Wall Street, and at top universities.

Breach of Trust

Perhaps Dawkins's most egregious and destructive polemical device is his breach of trust with the reader. Readers of Dawkins are usually not experts in science and religion. When a reader

19. The Latin phrase *abusus non tollit usum* applies here: "abuse does not preclude proper use."

20. For example, Dawkins tries to use the Westboro Baptist Church and the "American Taliban" as representative examples.

picks up a book of nonfiction, there is an implicit trust given to the author. We seek truth. We expect fairness, unless the author explicitly claims to be unfair at the outset. We assume his aim is to be objective. We would like to think that the author has been thorough. Dawkins consistently fails to meet these expectations, and the insult and injury done to the reader is impossible to overlook.

Although we expect an author to be knowledgeable, no reader expects perfection, so mistakes, omissions, and the occasional missed fact are understandable. However, Dawkins stretches his ignorance and naïveté to the point of disbelief by failing to make a good-faith effort at research. For example, he declares, "Much of the Bible is not systematically evil but just plain weird, as you would expect of a chaotically cobbled-together anthology of disjointed documents, composed, revised, translated, distorted and 'improved' by hundreds of anonymous authors."[21] Much of what Dawkins says here is demonstrably false, as a little research would show, but again Dawkins ignores the many thorough and thoughtful treatments of the subject.[22] A simple reading of the Bible would demonstrate that many biblical authors identify themselves *in the text* and can therefore hardly be described as "anonymous."[23]

21. Dawkins, *The God Delusion*, 268.

22. For a few examples, see Edward J. Young, *Thy Word Is Truth* (London: Banner of Truth, 1963); Benjamin Breckinridge Warfield, *The Inspiration and Authority of the Bible* (Philadelphia: Presbyterian and Reformed, 1948); John Frame, *The Doctrine of the Word of God* (Phillipsburg, NJ: P&R Publishing, 2010).

23. In another example, atheist Christopher Hitchens asserts, "The contradictions and illiteracies of the New Testament have filled up many books by eminent scholars and have never been explained by any Christian authority except in the feeblest terms of 'metaphor' and 'a Christ of faith'" (Hitchens, *God Is Not Great*, 115). I spent thirty seconds on Google and found the following two compendiums of answers for these "contradictions": *The Big Book of Bible Difficulties*, by Geisler and Howe, and the *New International Encyclopedia of Bible Difficulties*, by Archer. One wonders how Hitchens could have overlooked such evidence. In addition, Hitchens cites no references for his

Semantic Considerations

The Question of Faith

Redefining and using words in ways Christians would not use them is a misleading tactic that Dawkins uses frequently. He causes chaos in the process. Words form the basis of any discussion; therefore, precision is essential. If two people use the same word, but mean different things, then comprehension and communication become extremely difficult. We have already seen this in how Dawkins uses the word "religion." He also consistently wields the words "faith," "belief," "evidence," "fact," "proof," and "reason" in unclear, inconsistent ways.[24]

Let us start with a few examples, so we can be on the lookout for this misdirection. Dawkins writes, "A case can be made that faith is one of the world's great evils, comparable to the smallpox virus but harder to eradicate. Faith, being belief that isn't based on evidence, is the principal vice of any religion."[25] He continues in *The God Delusion*, "Faith is an evil precisely because it requires no justification and brooks no argument."[26] "Scientific belief is based upon publicly checkable evidence. Religious faith not only lacks evidence, its independence from evidence is its joy, shouted from the rooftops."[27]

This last quote is particularly telling because it purports to distinguish between belief and faith. Yet many dictionaries would

---

claim. Is he deliberately suppressing evidence, which would have severe implications for the trustworthiness of his position—or just abandoning objectivity altogether, which also affects his credibility?

24. For more on Dawkins's misuse of words, see Alister McGrath, *Dawkins' God: Genes, Memes and the Meaning of Life* (Malden, MA: Blackwell Publishing, 2005), 82–91.

25. Richard Dawkins, "Is Science a Religion?," *The Humanist*, January-February 1997, 26–39.

26. Dawkins, *The God Delusion*, 347.

27. Richard Dawkins, in the *Daily Telegraph Science Extra*, September 11, 1989.

describe the words as synonymous. However, there is an interesting substitution here. Most dictionaries actually use a different word in place of "evidence." Dictionary.com defines faith as "belief that is not based on proof." Merriam-Webster online defines it as follows: "firm belief in something for which there is no proof." Dawkins and the New Atheists have interchanged "evidence" and "proof." Most Christians would readily admit that they cannot *prove* God's existence, but they could present strong evidence to support their faith. There is a "critical distinction between the 'total absence of supporting evidence' and the 'absence of totally supporting evidence.'"[28] This usage of the word "faith" "is not a Christian definition of faith but one that Dawkins has invented to suit his own polemical purposes."[29] Criminal lawyers would spot this discrepancy immediately and poke holes in the argument. Finding someone's DNA at a crime scene provides evidence for their culpability, but does not prove their guilt.[30]

In fact, Gödel's Second Incompleteness Theorem proves that we can't prove everything. That is, we all (Dawkins included) believe some things without proof, but this does not mean that we believe things without evidence.[31] Dawkins has failed to distinguish between *types* of belief: belief supported by evidence, belief without evidence, and belief despite a preponderance of contrary evidence.

The Bible seeks to show supporting evidence and encourages believers to seek it out. "Now Jesus did many other signs in the

28. Alister McGrath, *Why God Won't Go Away* (Nashville: Thomas Nelson, 2010), 111.

29. Alister E. McGrath and Joanna Collicutt McGrath, *The Dawkins Delusion?* (Downers Grove, IL: InterVarsity Press, 2007), 17. Here Dawkins uses a straw man argument.

30. For more on Dawkins's idea of "faith," see John Lennox, *Gunning for God: Why the New Atheists Are Missing the Target* (Oxford: Lion Hudson, 2011), 37–41.

31. See George Boolos, "Gödel's Second Incompleteness Theorem Explained in Words of One Syllable," *Mind* 103 (1994): 1–3.

presence of his disciples, which are not written in this book; but these are written so that you may believe that Jesus is the Christ" (John 20:30–31). We should always have a reason for the hope that is in us (1 Peter 3:15).[32] Nowhere does Christianity encourage people to abandon their brains in order to believe. John Lennox writes:

> Faith is not something that makes up for a lack of evidence, so that strength of faith is inversely proportional to strength of evidence. Nor is faith that which "supports beliefs that lack the ordinary support of evidence or argument." It is the other way round, as we all surely know very well. The more evidence I see for trusting a document or a person, the stronger will be my trust in it or her.[33]

In fact, Dawkins nullified his own argument in a debate with John Lennox in 2007:

> Dawkins: We only need to use the word "faith" when there isn't any evidence.
> Lennox: No, not at all. I presume you've got faith in your wife—is there any evidence for that?
> Dawkins: Yes, plenty of evidence.[34]

Here Dawkins admits that his faith in his wife is partly due to evidence supporting that faith. In light of this, it seems we can ignore much of Dawkins's railing against faith and concentrate

32. See also John 13:19; 14:29; 16:4.

33. Lennox, *Gunning for God*, 42. He quotes Julian Baggini, *Atheism—A Very Short Introduction* (Oxford: Oxford University Press, 2003), 33.

34. "The God Delusion Debate," held at the University of Alabama at Birmingham, October 3, 2007, part I, 36.20. Transcript available at http://www.protorah.com /god-delusion-debate-dawkins-lennox-transcript/.

on the real issue: evidence. Dawkins claims, "The dictionary supplied with Microsoft Word defines a delusion as 'a persistent false belief held in the face of strong contradictory evidence, especially as a symptom of psychiatric disorder'. The first part captures religious faith perfectly."[35] Here is the real question: is there evidence for God or strong contradictory evidence?

---

35. Dawkins, *The God Delusion*, 28.

6

EVIDENCE AND WORLDVIEW

On the issue of evidence, a squabble erupts. Christians say they have evidence for God; Dawkins says he has "strong contradictory evidence." How are we to determine the truth? What constitutes evidence? Who decides? How much is determined by how we approach the evidence? What we believe at the start—our preconceptions and presuppositions—influences how we acquire and examine evidence. How we examine evidence affects how decisions are made, which then affects behavior. Initial assumptions affect final outcomes. Our beliefs have consequences, and some beliefs are false. For example, simply believing that arsenic will not kill me would not prevent me from dying if I consumed it. Two people examining the same evidence through different interpretative lenses can arrive at different conclusions. Therefore, before we can look at evidence, we must examine how evidence is weighed and assessed.

The Question of Evidence

At its root, the question of evidence is a worldview problem: the issues trace back to truth and how we acquire it. The grand misconception is that science is the only way to truth. The hallowed scientific method is often regarded as an unbiased truth finder, and it *has* revealed true things. It has helped correct misconceptions, like the belief in a geocentric universe. However, just because we can learn truth from science, it does not follow that *all* truth comes from science. Nor does science create truth; it merely discovers and describes truths that are already there.

These distortions and misconceptions arise when we assume that science "proclaims" truth. Science itself does not say anything. It does not speak or make proclamations. As Lennox puts it, "Statements by scientists are not necessarily statements of science. Nor, we might add, are such statements necessarily true; although the prestige of science is such that they are often taken to be so."[1] People perform scientific experiments and interpret data to support their theories, and because people are flawed, interpretations can be erroneous. People can never be entirely objective.[2] In fact, one of the hallmarks of the scientific method and its claim to objective integrity is the test of reproducibility and repeatability. Yet, when people actually try to duplicate findings, the results are sometimes abysmal.[3] Here is a helpful visual of Dawkins's interpretation of science, beginning with nature alone:

1. John Lennox, *God's Undertaker: Has Science Buried God?* (Oxford: Lion Hudson, 2009), 19.

2. Yet the claims of objectivity are fiercely protected, for "if a scientist . . . has a personal stake in his or her discovery, its veracity is automatically suspect" (Elaine Howard Ecklund, *Science vs. Religion: What Scientists Really Think* [Oxford: Oxford University Press, 2010], 7). Acknowledging the effects of preexisting suppositions and worldviews is thought to undermine the claims of science. Yet this is a problem only if scientists are the source of the truth of science. If God is the source of truth, then we have no problem humbly admitting our own failings and biases.

3. A. A. Aarts et al., "Estimating the Reproducibility of Psychological Science," *Science* 349, no. 6251 (August 28, 2015). Accessed online at http://science.science mag.org/content/349/6251/aac4716.

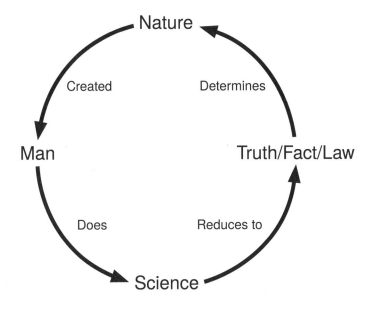

Fig. 6.1. Science without God

As you can see, this circular thinking puts humans in charge, which is a risky thing to do, especially given our known propensity to inaccuracy, selfishness, and sinful imperfection. Humans discover, decide, and define truth. But there is no good reason why we should trust that our reasoning is actually revealing truth. Why does our reasoning work? As C. S. Lewis puts it, "If the value of our reasoning is in doubt, you cannot try to establish it by reasoning."[4] However, truth and reason *will* function if they are established and upheld by God. In an effort to wed science and God, many well-meaning but misguided Christians have tried to fold this perspective into Christian belief, like so:

4. C. S. Lewis, *Miracles* (1947; New York: HarperCollins, 1996), 33.

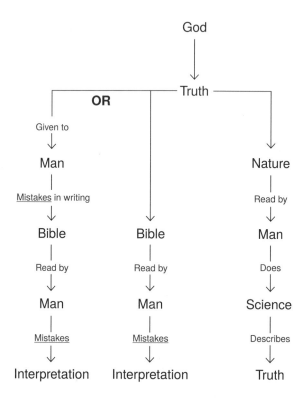

Fig. 6.2. Theology in Service to Science

In this view, God is the source of truth, but mankind has to use his best judgment to extract truth from the Bible, since it is riddled with human error. But that same human error will extend to our efforts to extract truth! Yet, in this way of thinking, truth is still perfectly revealed in science, since this view upholds science as a purely objective process. This flawed position is too quick to capitulate to man's interpretation of science. It fails to acknowledge that science is a human enterprise and therefore fallible and subject to error, like every human endeavor. Although nature, as God's creation, cannot lie or tell an untruth, we can misinterpret what we see. We can even pursue questions and answers to confirm what we already believe, turning a blind eye to other possibilities.[5] This happens even in peer-reviewed, published studies, where scientists admit to being "totally blinded by our belief."[6] The true Christian will submit to God and his truth, even if it is in conflict with his own desires. The Christian perspective will look more like this:

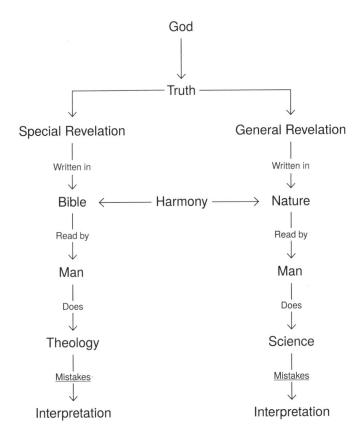

Fig. 6.3. Theology and Science in Harmony

5. For a review, see Raymond S. Nickerson, "Confirmation Bias: A Ubiquitous Phenomenon in Many Guises," *Review of General Psychology* 2, no. 2 (June 1998): 175–220. For a more recent example in biology, see Jonathan Wells, *The Myth of Junk DNA* (Seattle: Discovery Institute Press, 2011).

6. Jack Szostak on the retraction of *Nature Chemistry* paper "Oligoarginine

This perspective gives Christians both confidence and humility: confidence because we know that truth exists and that God actively reveals it to us, and humility because we are flawed, corrupt, and finite. We are not the arbiters of truth. God is the source of all truth and has promised in Scripture to perfectly preserve truth as revealed in the Bible and in nature (Isa. 40:8; Matt. 5:18; 2 Tim. 3:16). This perspective also clarifies another essential truth: the Bible and creation are not in conflict. There is no war between genuine science and genuine religion.[7] Sometimes our interpretation of the Bible and our interpretation of creation through science can *seem* to be in conflict, but we know that the conflict is just a product of our finite, flawed nature.

Another important clarification needs to be made at this point. Although it appears that theology and science run along two separate, nonintersecting paths, the reality is that there can only be one truth, from God. The truth we seek from the Bible and from the study of science is the same: truth that derives from God. Science and theology complement and harmonize with each other. The Bible and nature cannot be in conflict because God cannot be in conflict with himself. Dealing with this perspective means we need to understand a little more about the worldviews that tell us how we get our "facts" or "evidence." We circle back to the critical question: how do we arrive at knowledge and ascertain truth?

Peptides Slow Strand Annealing and Assist Nonenzymatic RNA Replication." Accessed online at https://retractionwatch.com/2017/12/05/definitely-embarrassing-nobel-laureate-retracts-non-reproducible-paper-nature-journal/#more-52894.

7. For more on this, see Alister McGrath, *Dawkins' God: Genes, Memes and the Meaning of Life* (Malden, MA: Blackwell Publishing, 2005), chap. 5, and John Lennox, *God's Undertaker: Has Science Buried God?* (Oxford: Lion Hudson, 2009), 23–28.

The Question of Worldview

When discussing worldviews with others, we need to identify the underlying assumptions. An essential question is, "Are the initial assumptions supported by the reasoning that follows from them? Or are the assumptions self-refuting?" Put another way, "Does a worldview form a vicious or virtuous cycle of reasoning?"

Self-Refutation and Assumptions[8]

Let us look at a few simple examples. The sentence "This statement is false" is a self-refuting statement. If the sentence is true, it means that the sentence is false. It cannot be both true and false at the same time. There are other such easily identifiable self-refuting statements: "There are no absolute truths" and "I do not exist."

As we move into the scientific realm, the conversation can become trickier. For example, William Clifford once said, "It is wrong always, everywhere, and for anyone to believe anything upon insufficient evidence."[9] There is not sufficient evidence, however, for his statement; therefore, it is self-refuting.

Yet we see eminent scientists saying essentially the same thing: scientism declares that science is the only way to know truth—yet this statement is not verifiable by science! "Whatever knowledge is attainable, must be attained by scientific methods; and what science cannot discover, mankind cannot know."[10] And again, "There is no reason to suppose that science cannot

8. For more on self-refutation, see http://frame-poythress.org/self-refuting -statements/.

9. Michael Peterson, William Hasker, Bruce Reichenbach, and David Basinger, eds., *Philosophy of Religion*, 3rd ed. (Oxford: Oxford University Press, 2007), 109. Clifford's essay appears on pages 104–10.

10. Bertrand Russell, *Religion and Science* (Oxford: Oxford University Press, 1970), 243.

deal with every aspect of existence. Only the religious—among whom I include not only the prejudiced but the uninformed—hope there is a dark corner of the physical universe, or of the universe of experience, that science can never hope to illuminate."[11]

In order for these assertions to be true, they themselves must be false, since science cannot provide evidence for their validity.[12] Hence, scientism is self-contradictory. It forms a vicious circle. John Haught sums it up nicely:[13]

> Scientism tells us to take nothing on faith, and yet faith is required to accept scientism. What is remarkable is that none of the new atheists seem remotely prepared to admit that his scientism is a self-sabotaging confession of faith. Listen to Hitchens: "If one must have faith in order to believe in something, then the likelihood of that something having any truth or value is considerably diminished." But this statement invalidates itself since it too arises out of faith in things unseen. There is no set of tangible experiments or visible demonstrations that could ever scientifically prove the statement to be true. In order to issue the just-quoted pronouncement with such confidence, Hitchens already has to have subscribed to the creed of a faith community for which scientism and scientific naturalism provide the dogmatic substance.[14]

Dawkins and other atheists have worldviews, just as we all do. There are no exceptions among humans. The difficulty comes

11. Peter Atkins, *Nature's Imagination: The Frontiers of Scientific Vision*, ed. John Cornwell (Oxford: Oxford University Press, 1995), 125.

12. For more, see Gregory R. Peterson, "Demarcation and the Scientistic Fallacy," *Zygon: Journal of Religion and Science*, 38 (December 9, 2003): 751–61.

13. See also Lennox, *God's Undertaker*, 43, on the self-contradiction of scientism.

14. John F. Haught, *God and the New Atheism* (Louisville: Westminster John Knox, 2008), 17. He quotes Christopher Hitchens, *God Is Not Great: How Religion Poisons Everything* (New York: Twelve Books, 2007), 71.

because they either refuse to admit that they have worldviews or refuse to acknowledge that their worldviews may be faulty. Dawkins, like the rest of us, is not philosophically neutral.

For example, Dawkins writes,

> The vast majority of theological writings simply assume that [God exists] and go on from there. For my purposes, I need consider only those theologians who take seriously the possibility that God does not exist.[15]

Try rephrasing this, and put the worldview of naturalism in the place of God:

> The vast majority of *scientific writings* simply assume that *naturalism* is true and go on from there. For my purposes, I need consider only those *scientists* who take seriously the possibility that *naturalism* may be wrong.

Dawkins has started with a philosophical assumption about the truth of naturalism. Is that assumption supported?

We will not be so cavalier as to dismiss Dawkins's beliefs just because he starts with an assumption. We will examine his worldview and the beliefs that follow from it and see if his faith assumption is justified: "Scientific rationalists consider that the many successes of science fully justify them in holding this faith with absolute certainty. Indeed, they consider that faith in scientific naturalism is so thoroughly justified by reason that they do not think of it as a faith but as a defining example of reason."[16]

15. Richard Dawkins, *The God Delusion* (New York: Houghton Mifflin, 2006, 2008), 14.

16. Phillip E. Johnson and John Mark Reynolds, *Against All Gods: What's Right and Wrong about the New Atheism* (Downers Grove, IL: InterVarsity Press, 2010), 34–35.

Naturalism

I have already used the words *naturalism* and *scientism*, but Dawkins's worldview can also be described as materialism, methodological naturalism, Darwinism, evolutionism, secularism, and humanism. There are various subtleties. In conversation, different people may use these words differently, and we should ask them for clarity. But for our purposes, to quote Dawkins himself:

> An atheist in this sense of philosophical naturalist is somebody who believes there is nothing beyond the natural, physical world, no supernatural creative intelligence lurking behind the observable universe, no soul that outlasts the body and no miracles—except in the sense of natural phenomena that we don't yet understand. If there is something that appears to lie beyond the natural world as it is now imperfectly understood, we hope eventually to understand it and embrace it within the natural.[17]

In accordance with his own definition of naturalism, Dawkins excludes anything supernatural. If naturalism is true, then God, if he existed, would have to be determinable and definable by natural means, which would not really make him supernatural. Or, stated the other way, by definition God cannot exist, because if he did, we would not be able to understand him, which would falsify naturalism.[18] As Richard Lewontin admits:

> Our willingness to accept scientific claims that are against

17. Dawkins, *The God Delusion*, 35.
18. Cf. C. F. von Weizsäcker: "It is not by its conclusions but by its methodological starting point that modern science excludes direct creation. Our methodology would not be honest if this fact were denied . . . . Such is the faith in the science of our time, and which we all share" (*The Relevance of Science* [New York: Collins, 1964], 136).

common sense is the key to an understanding of the real strug-
gle between science and the supernatural. We take the side
of science in spite of the patent absurdity of some of its con-
structs . . . in spite of the tolerance of the scientific community for unsubstantiated just-so stories, because we have a prior
commitment . . . to materialism. It is not that the methods and
institutions of science somehow compel us to accept a material explanation of the phenomenal world but, on the contrary,
that we are forced by our a priori adherence to material causes
to create an apparatus of investigation and a set of concepts
that produce material explanations, no matter how counter-
intuitive, no matter how mystifying to the uninitiated.[19]

This commitment is dogmatic and unshakeable. Dawkins
himself confesses his religious adherence: "Even if there were
no actual evidence in favour of Darwinism (there is, of course)
we should still be justified in preferring it over all rival theories."[20]

It sometimes sounds like Dawkins might be convinced of
God if *positive* evidence existed: "If all the evidence in the universe turned in favour of creationism, I would be the first to
admit it, and I would immediately change my mind."[21] But then
he asserts that no such evidence *could* exist:

Scientists of a rationalist bent are often challenged to say what
might in principle cause them to change their minds and come
to regard naturalism as falsified. What would it take to convince
you of something supernatural? I used to pay lip service to the
promise that I would become a supernaturalist overnight, the

19. Richard Lewontin, "Billions and Billions of Demons," *New York Times Book Review* (January 9, 1997), 31.

20. Richard Dawkins, *The Blind Watchmaker* (New York: W. W. Norton, 1986), 287.

21. Dawkins, *The God Delusion*, 19.

moment somebody showed me some convincing evidence. But now . . . I am less sure. . . . Why would I reject the hypothesis that I was dreaming, or hallucinating, or the victim of a cunning illusion. . . . What could supernatural even mean, other than falling outside our present, temporarily imperfect understanding of science? . . . We should exercise the same skepticism over all alleged miracles because the alternative to the miracle hypothesis, even though implausible, is nevertheless more plausible than the miracle.[22]

Here he confesses that his worldview affects how he interprets the evidence.

Once we have defined Dawkins's naturalism, we must decide if it is a justifiable worldview. Is there anything that is not explainable by natural means? It is convenient to say that anything that is not explainable now will be explainable later (a "god of the gaps" argument). However, it is possible that the very definition of naturalism asserts certain things as unexplainable, thus nullifying the legitimacy of the worldview. In other words, is naturalism itself supported by natural means?[23] We will briefly examine one argument along those lines.

The EAAN: The Evolutionary Argument against Naturalism

The EAAN was popularized by philosopher Alvin Plantinga in 1993 in his book *Warrant and Proper Function* (although there were earlier formulations of it, including one by C. S. Lewis).

22. Richard Dawkins, *Brief Candle in the Dark: My Life in Science* (London: Bantam, 2015), 202–3.

23. Abstract concepts, such as logic and consciousness, pose significant difficulties for naturalism. Even the concept of naturalism itself cannot be defined within the confines of naturalism.

The argument proceeds roughly as follows: If naturalism is true and evolution describes how life came to be, then life is driven by adaptive survival advantage and not by truth. As philosopher Patricia Churchland puts it, "Truth, whatever that is, definitely takes the hindmost."[24] In other words, our bodies are survival machines and tell us whatever is necessary to help us adapt and survive, even if it is false. In fact, there is a high probability that our bodies are telling us falsehoods in order to help us survive.[25] Most of what we know may be false, since evolution does not support truth, but only adaptation. Therefore, there is no reason to suppose that naturalism itself is true, since there is a greater probability that we just believe it to be true to help us survive. In other words, if naturalism is true, then we have no reason to trust what we believe as being true, including the statement that naturalism is true. As John Piper puts it, "Atheistic man uses his mind to create a worldview that nullifies the use of his mind."[26]

That may sound a bit confusing, so here is an example of how it might play out. If naturalism and evolutionary theory are true, then our goal/purpose is to propagate our genes. However, I am guessing you do not feel or act like propagation is your primary purpose. This means either that we are deceiving ourselves and are being tricked by our very own bodies into *thinking* we have purpose outside of reproduction (like a puppet on a string) or that naturalism is not to be trusted. If we are being deceived by our genes, can we rebel and act against them? Dawkins believes

24. Patricia Smith Churchland, "Epistemology in the Age of Neuroscience," *The Journal of Philosophy* 84, no. 10 (October 1987): 549.
25. It is difficult to assess this probability precisely.
26. John Piper, "C. S. Lewis, Romantic Rationalist: How His Paths to Christ Shaped His Life and Ministry," from a 2013 conference on "The Romantic Rationalist: God, Life, and Imagination in the Work of C. S. Lewis," September 27, 2013. Accessed online at http://www.desiringgod.org/messages/c-s-lewis-romantic-rationalist-how-his-paths-to-christ-shaped-his-life-and-ministry.

we can.[27] We feel like we can resist our impulses and make independent personal choices. If that is true, then naturalism is wrong, since it has no real power to trick or deceive. "To posit a free-willed agent . . . is to insert into a physical system a physical being that is no longer solely reacting in response to that physical system. This necessarily creates rippling effects that are unpredictable by physical (naturalistic) explanation, and therefore cuts [naturalistic] assumptions off at the knees."[28] If, on the other hand, personal choice is false, then all of our choosing is an illusion and we are being manipulated and programmed by an external mindless force. This is dangerous ground to tread, because a direct consequence of choice being an illusion would be that people cannot be held morally accountable for criminal behavior.[29]

27. "Let us understand what our own selfish genes are up to, because we may then at least have a chance to upset their designs." Dawkins, *Selfish Gene*, 3.

28. Wayne Rossiter, *Shadow of Oz* (Eugene, OR: Pickwick Publications, 2015), 76.

29. There continues to be a good deal of discussion surrounding the EAAN without any conclusive consensus. A number of philosophers wrote essays objecting to the EAAN, and they were published in 2002 as *Naturalism Defeated?* with Plantinga writing responses to those objections. Plantinga again published a version of the EAAN in *Where the Conflict Really Lies* (2011).

7

ISSUES IN SCIENCE

Since nature itself is created and sustained by God (Col. 1:16–17), Christians can confidently and wholeheartedly pursue science in the world that he has made. However, science as a human endeavor is interpretive and can be flawed. As we have seen, the conclusions drawn from science become problematic when science is considered the only standard of truth. As mentioned previously, Dawkins has begun leaning heavily on some of the new findings from science in order to argue his case.

The core question for much of this chapter is: how did it all start? Without the sovereign, creative genius of God, Dawkins cannot explain how things originated. Although the literature on these topics is extensive, in this chapter we will discuss some of the shortcomings of Dawkins's forays into scientific issues.

The Origin of Origins

What started it all? Go far enough back, and what was the first "thing"? This is something of a philosophical question, but it nicely bridges the gap between worldview and science. To support their view that God started it all, theists sometimes use what is known as the cosmological argument, which has taken various forms through the ages. Although it is not a "proof" of God in a final sense, it is "to be seen as a demonstration of the inner coherence of belief in God."[1] A highly simplified version is as follows:[2]

1. Everything that begins to exist has a cause.
2. Nothing can cause itself (no causal loops).
3. You cannot have an infinite regress of causes (a cause that has a cause, which has a cause, ad infinitum).
4. Therefore, there must be a First Cause that has no beginning.[3]

Some common objections to the cosmological argument include saying that the universe itself is the first cause. That is, it just is.[4] Others object that this argument is a form of special pleading: why can't we demand a cause for God? As Dawkins puts it, "The whole argument turns on the familiar question 'Who made God?', which most thinking people discover for themselves."[5]

The naturalistic worldview clearly comes into play here and affects the discussion. Nature, as studied by scientists, is a lot about causation: how physical or chemical alterations cause

1. Alister E. McGrath and Joanna Collicutt McGrath, *The Dawkins Delusion?* (Downers Grove, IL: InterVarsity Press, 2007), 26.

2. For a more technical formulation and handling, see William Lane Craig, "The Existence of God and the Beginning of the Universe," *Truth: A Journal of Modern Thought* 3 (1991): 85–96. Accessed online at http://www.leaderu.com/truth/3truth11.html.

3. It should be noted that the argument doesn't make any claims about God specifically or what he might be like.

4. Bertrand Russell and Frederick Copleston, "Debate on the Existence of God," in *The Existence of God*, ed. John Hick (New York: Macmillan, 1964), 175.

5. Richard Dawkins, *The God Delusion* (New York: Houghton Mifflin, 2006, 2008), 136.

changes. In fact, we can almost define something as "natural" if it has a cause—if it is contingent. Infinite regresses of causation are problematic for natural causes because they are by definition limited by natural law. If something is natural, it must have a cause. If the Big Bang is "natural" in the sense of involving matter, then it must have a cause and we are legitimately allowed to ask what caused the existence of the universe. The only thing that does not demand a cause is something that is not natural. God is not natural. He is not contingent. God is supernatural. Causation and contingency are not necessary parts of the supernatural. God cannot be explained by contingent things like matter and atoms because he himself is not contingent. Therefore, by the very rules of nature and naturalism, we have every right to demand an explanation for a contingent event like the Big Bang, but we cannot ask the same question of God.[6]

Dawkins wades into this discussion swinging his naturalistic presuppositions like a blind prize fighter: "A designer God cannot be used to explain organized complexity because any God capable of designing anything would have to be complex enough to demand the same kind of explanation in his own right."[7] Dawkins continues:

> I challenged the theologians to answer the point that a God capable of designing a universe, or anything else, would have to be complex and statistically improbable. . . . Scientific arguments, such as those I was accustomed to deploying in my own field, were inappropriate since theologians had always maintained that God lay outside science. . . . The theologians

6. For more on nature, God, and contingency, see Keith Ward, *Why There Almost Certainly Is a God* (Oxford: Lion Hudson, 2008), 47 and 54. Furthermore, the universe must exist within the constraints of time, whereas God, who created time, is not bound by it in the same way that nature is bound.

7. Dawkins, *The God Delusion*, 136.

... were defining themselves into an epistemological Safe Zone where rational argument could not reach them because they had declared by fiat that it could not. Who was I to say that rational argument was the only admissible kind of argument? There are other ways of knowing besides the scientific, and it is one of these other ways of knowing that must be deployed to know God. . . . God . . . cannot be, whatever else he might be, simple. . . . God may not have a brain made of neurons, or a CPU made of silicon, but if he has the powers attributed to him he must have something far more elaborately and non-randomly constructed than the largest brain or the largest computer we know. . . . The first cause that we seek must have been the simple basis for a self-bootstrapping crane which eventually raised the world as we know it into its present complex existence.[8]

This is, in many respects, a stunning section of writing, rife with problematic assertions that necessarily flow from Dawkins's naturalistic assumptions. Dawkins demands God's "complexity" have an explanation and insists that any explanation fit within our own finite understanding. This is a little like asking an ant to explain quantum mechanics. The ant is incapable of such a task, but that does not make quantum mechanics untrue. Dawkins wants to limit God to the world of science and naturalism. Dawkins has no rationale or justification for saying that God must be *within* the purview of science. He just declares it.

Notice how Dawkins equates science with rationality, and religion with irrational superstition. Nowhere does he provide any justification for doing this. He just assumes that science is rational and that it is the only rational thing. We have shown above how this kind of scientism is actually self-refuting. His sentence looks less intimidating if "rational" is not unjustifiably

8. Ibid., 183–85.

replaced by "scientific": "Who was I to say that scientific argument was the only admissible kind of argument?"

Dawkins's solution to the "first cause" question is a "self-bootstrapping crane," which is another name for a causal loop: something that causes itself to exist. Nothing like this is known to exist or ever to have existed in the natural world: it is purely hypothetical and speculative.

The cosmological argument and the question of first causes continues to be discussed by philosophers on both sides, but hopefully we have provided some justification for its serious consideration and shown that it is not so easily discarded as Dawkins would have the reader believe.

The Origin of Law and Rationality

Naturalism, by definition, requires that all things have natural explanations. However, the existence and intelligibility of nature itself has no natural explanation. Dawkins cannot explain the explicability of the world. "The more scientific advance is achieved, the greater will be our understanding of the universe—and hence the greater need to explain this very success."[9]

How are things explainable? How is truth attainable? By science and the scientific method! Scientists start with the scientific method as an objective, unbiased purveyor of truth that supposedly involves no faith. But they forget that they must have faith in the method! "Just because the sun has risen every day of your life, there is no guarantee that it will therefore rise tomorrow. The belief that it will—that there are indeed dependable regularities of nature—is an act of faith, but one which is indispensable to the progress of science."[10]

9. McGrath and McGrath, *The Dawkins Delusion?*, 31.
10. Paul Davies, *The Mind of God: The Scientific Basis for a Rational World* (New York: Simon & Schuster, 1992), 81.

Indeed, in order for science to proceed, "scientists have to believe in the rational intelligibility of the universe as their fundamental article of faith or basic assumption."[11] In other words, reality cannot be an illusion and our senses must be reliable. The universe itself must be orderly and understandable for science to proceed. But why is the universe orderly and understandable? The rationality of the universe cannot be described, explained, or derived from natural principles. There is no reason why the universe is rational. There is no reason that laws of any kind should exist in the first place and no plausible scenario for where they came from. In this view, there is no good reason for our world being reasonable![12]

"Professor Sir John Polkinghorne points out: 'physics is powerless to explain its faith [note his explicit use of the word] in the mathematical intelligibility of the universe', for the simple reason that you cannot begin to do physics without believing in that intelligibility."[13] Einstein even said, "The most incomprehensible thing about the universe is that it is comprehensible."[14] The functionality of naturalism cannot be explained by naturalism. This is a vicious circle because naturalism demands (by its own rules) that it be able to explain itself.

Take, for example, the origin of scientific laws. Where did the

11. John Lennox, *Gunning for God: Why the New Atheists Are Missing the Target* (Oxford: Lion Hudson, 2011), 49.

12. Yet, "unless human reasoning is valid no science can be true" (C. S. Lewis, *Miracles* [1947; New York: HarperCollins, 1996], 21). "No one doubts that the equations work, but *why* do they work? And why can we figure them out, and why do they make sense to us? Questions like these had clear answers back when science grew within the Christian tradition: God is the Creator. He created the universe to work in regular ways, and we can understand these patterns because we are made in his image" (John Bloom, *The Natural Sciences: A Student's Guide* [Wheaton, IL: Crossway, 2015], 72–73).

13. Lennox, *Gunning for God*, 50.

14. Albert Einstein, "Physics and Reality" (1936), in *Ideas and Opinions*, trans. Sonja Bargmann (New York: Bonanza, 1954), 292.

law of gravity come from? Victor Stenger tries to say that natural law arises from "universe symmetries," but he has not actually solved anything, for where did the symmetries come from? He answers: "So where did the laws of physics come from? They came from nothing! Most are statements composed by humans that follow from the symmetries of the void out of which the universe spontaneously arose."[15] In other words, we can describe the symmetries of the universe, but we cannot create them or explain their origin. There is no reason that there should be any symmetries to begin with. So scientists are left making nonsensical statements like "Because there is a law such as gravity, the universe can and will create itself from nothing."[16] But the fact is that law is not active. It does nothing. Scientific laws are merely human descriptions to help us approximate the future based on past performance. They only exist because something or someone outside of the law enforces it. Mitch Stokes makes the point in a different way:

> Newton's law of universal gravitation . . . describes the force between objects. . . . Yet this is "all" it does: it merely describes. . . . But his law doesn't tell us what *causes* the force; it doesn't *explain* the objects' behavior. It doesn't answer the question *why is the force thus?*[17]

This quandary extends to more than just the law and rationality of the universe. There are many aspects of science that

15. Victor Stenger, *God: The Failed Hypothesis* (Amherst, NY: Prometheus Books, 2007), 131.

16. Michael Holden, "God Did Not Create the Universe, Says Hawking," *Reuters*, September 2, 2010. Accessed online at https://www.reuters.com/article /us-britain-hawking/god-did-not-create-the-universe-says-hawking-idUSTRE 6811FN20100902.

17. Mitch Stokes, *How to Be an Atheist: Why Many Skeptics Aren't Skeptical Enough* (Wheaton, IL: Crossway, 2016), 65.

cannot be explained by science. Vern Poythress points to several of these in *Redeeming Science*. Scientific laws are uniform—that is, they hold in all places in the universe at all times. They have not changed at any point in history. Or, to use a different set of descriptors, scientific law is omnipresent, eternal, and immutable. Why does scientific law have these characteristics?[18] Why aren't we in a universe that is constantly changing? How did "laws" come to be? There is no explanation, nor can there be from a purely naturalistic view. Naturalism demands that we be able to account for everything, yet we cannot. Theism does not make the same demands of mankind. There is an expectation that there will be mysterious things that are not comprehensible to finite human beings. If we could understand everything, we would be gods. If God really is supernatural, there will be things that we cannot understand or explain, but that does not mean that he cannot.

At this point, Dawkins might complain that the appeal to God ends inquiry and bankrupts science; however, this simply is not true. We do not understand everything, but because we desire to seek, know, and understand God, we do not stop trying.[19] We just humbly acknowledge our limitations. For example, physicists do not understand how light can be both a particle and a wave, but that has not stopped them from trying to figure it out or continuing to experiment, based on what they do know. In seeking to fulfill our creation mandate (Gen. 1:28), we never stop the journey of discovery!

In fact, the rationality of the world can tell us something about God: the truth, immanence, power, and harmonies of the world match what we know about the God of the Bible. "For what can be known about God is plain to them, because God has

18. These are the very characteristics of God, whose fingerprint we would expect to see on his creation.

19. Prov. 25:2: "It is the glory of God to conceal things, but the glory of kings is to search things out."

shown it to them. For his invisible attributes, namely, his eternal power and divine nature, have been clearly perceived, ever since the creation of the world, in the things that have been made. So they are without excuse" (Rom. 1:19–20). The God of the Bible provides an explanation, not only for why science works, but also for why it works this particular way. Naturalism has no natural explanation for why science works, and yet it demands that explanation.

The Origin of Our Universe

As we have discussed, it is satisfactory to claim that God created the universe and then seek to use the tools of science in accord with God's revelation to probe how he might have accomplished that. Dawkins has a quandary on his hands at this point. Because of his commitment to naturalism, he needs an explanation for how the universe got here, and not just any universe, but this specific one. Beyond simply explaining why the world is rational, he must explain why it is rational in our particular way. He must not only explain why basic physical constants exist at all, but also why the constants are set at the specific values we see.

The fine-tuning argument proposes that the existence of God is necessary to explain the special circumstances of our universe. There are several universal constants (like the gravitation force or the strong nuclear force) which, had they been different, would make life impossible.[20] Why are these constants set so perfectly? How can Dawkins explain such an improbable

---

20. Stephen Hawking puts it this way: "Our universe and its laws appear to have a design that both is tailor-made to support us and, if we are to exist, leaves little room for alteration. That is not easily explained and raises the natural question of why it is that way" (Stephen Hawking and Leonard Mlodinow, *The Grand Design* [New York: Bantam, 2010], 164).

event?[21] He might say that the laws of nature had to be this way. They are constrained. Constrained by what? Such a constraint merely means that there is another set of laws that constrains the universe's existence. Where did those laws come from? What (or who) finely tuned those laws? It is a little like looking at our universe as an ice cube and asking why it appears so carefully crafted. Is it simply because it is constrained by the ice cube tray? But then we need to explain the careful design and creation of the ice cube tray itself.[22]

A common tack at this point is an appeal to the "multiverse." In essence, it admits that the universe in which we live is special, but then argues that if there are a very large number of universes in existence (perhaps an infinite number), then the probability of *our* universe coming into existence is very high.[23] Dawkins explains:

> The objection can be answered by the suggestion . . . that there are many universes, co-existing like bubbles of foam, in a 'multiverse'. . . . The laws and constants of any one universe,

21. Some atheists say this is a trivial question. Because we are here, they say, the universe had to be this way. Notice that this gets the question confused. The question is not "What's the probability that, since we are here, there is a finely tuned universe?" Rather, the question is "What's the probability of a finely tuned universe?" For further argument, see John Leslie, "Anthropic Principle, World Ensemble, Design," *American Philosophical Quarterly* 19, no. 2 (April 1982): 141–51; and Phil Dowe, *Galileo, Darwin, and Hawking* (Grand Rapids, MI: Eerdmans Publishing Company, 2005), 148–54.

22. For a fuller discussion of the fine-tuning argument, see Robin Collins, "A Scientific Argument for the Existence of God: The Fine-Tuning Design Argument," in *Reason for the Hope Within*, ed. Michael J. Murray (Grand Rapids: Eerdmans, 1999), 47–75. See also Hugh Ross, "Anthropic Principle: A Precise Plan for Humanity," *Reasons to Believe*, January 1, 2002, http://www.reasons.org/articles/anthropic-principle-a-precise-plan-for-humanity.

23. Some have argued that, even if true, the multiverse proposition still doesn't deal with the issue of universe uniqueness and improbability because it commits what is known as the Inverse Gambler's Fallacy. See Ian Hacking, "The Inverse Gambler's Fallacy: The Argument from Design. The Anthropic Principle Applied to Wheeler Universes," *Mind* 96 (1987): 331–40.

such as our observable universe, are by-laws. . . . The key difference between the genuinely extravagant God hypothesis and the apparently extravagant multiverse hypothesis is one of statistical improbability. The multiverse, for all that it is extravagant, is simple. God, or any intelligent, decision-taking, calculating agent, would have to be highly improbable in the very same statistical sense as the entities he is supposed to explain.[24]

As before, Dawkins's explanation is hardly convincing. Notice first that the multiverse theory is a suggestion. It is not science. It is untestable, unprovable, unverifiable speculation. You can believe it, but do not call it science. "People are uncomfortable with the purposefully created world. To come up with things that contradict purpose, they tend to speculate about things they haven't seen."[25]

Dawkins states that his multiverse hypothesis is simple, but who defines simplicity? He also implies that something simple is less improbable than something that is complex. He links this to his assertion that God is complex. "A God capable of continuously monitoring and controlling the individual status of every particle in the universe cannot be simple. His existence is going to need a mammoth explanation in its own right."[26] Notice that he simply makes this assertion. It will not be evident to others that an innumerable, perhaps infinite, number of universes operating under unlimited combinations of different rules sounds particularly simple.

Furthermore, Dawkins again demands a naturalistic explanation for God (in terms of material complexity), but that is

24. Dawkins, *The God Delusion*, 173–76.

25. Arno Penzias quoted in Denis Brian, *The Voice of Genius: Conversations with Nobel Scientists and Other Luminaries* (New York: Basic Books, 2000), 164.

26. Dawkins, *The God Delusion*, 178.

an explanatory burden that cannot be laid on the supernatural. Our scientific understanding of simplicity and complexity is entirely confined to the natural world. This essentially nullifies Dawkins's argument, since his argument about complexity cannot be extended to the supernatural; the category of "complex" belongs to the material, natural world. That is, we would expect a supernatural God to fall outside of our finite system of categorization.

This idea of simplicity has left the atheists like Dawkins grasping at thin air—or, to be precise, grasping at nothing at all: "Since 'nothing' is as simple as it gets, we cannot expect it to be very stable. It would likely undergo a spontaneous phase transition to something more complicated, like a universe containing matter. The transition of nothing-to-something is a natural one, not requiring any agent."[27] Even allowing for the existence of the multiverse, what about the finely tuned, particular laws controlling how universes come into existence? In other words, what about the rules governing multiverse generation? It is the ice cube question all over again.

We may ask for an explanation for the existence of the universe, and, in return, Dawkins may demand an explanation for the existence of God. Do both of these demands carry the same weight? Hopefully you can see that these demands are not equally justifiable.

The Origin of Life

The whole issue of origins is made clearer when we begin to examine not just the origin of the universe, but the origin of life. Dawkins describes it in oversimplifying, grandiose brush strokes that attempt to hide the gaping holes:

27. Stenger, *God: The Failed Hypothesis*, 133.

The origin of life was the chemical event, or series of events, whereby the vital conditions for natural selection first came about. The major ingredient was heredity, . . . something that copies like DNA but less accurately, perhaps the related molecule RNA. . . . The spontaneous arising by chance of the first hereditary molecule strikes many as improbable. Maybe it is— very very improbable. . . . However improbable the origin of life might be, we know it happened on Earth because we are here.[28]

It may be that the origin of life is not the only major gap in the evolutionary story that is bridged by sheer luck. . . . For example, [it has been] suggested that the origin of the eukaryotic cell . . . was an even more momentous, difficult and statistically improbable step than the origin of life. The origin of consciousness might be another major gap whose bridging was of the same order of improbability.[29]

Here we see a clear example of how limiting Dawkins's naturalistic presuppositions are. He has no other choice but to appeal to miraculous luck, since his worldview disallows supernatural input. In essence, the argument becomes: "It may seem improbable, but given enough chances, it becomes less improbable." "A billion billion is a conservative estimate of the number of available planets in the universe. Now, suppose the origin of life . . . really was a quite staggeringly improbable event. Suppose it was so improbable as to occur on only one in a billion planets . . . and yet . . . even with such absurdly long odds, life will still have arisen on a billion planets."[30]

The reader will notice that Dawkins proposes no explanation

28. Dawkins, *The God Delusion*, 164–65. See note 21 above for why this statement doesn't address the real question.

29. Ibid., 168.

30. Ibid., 165.

for how the first DNA-like molecule appeared and gives no justification for his assertion that the probability of life appearing is one in a billion. In fact, many estimates put the probability of randomly generating a single small peptide chain of 100 amino acids at 1 in 10^{125} (for reference, there are roughly 10^{85} particles in the entire universe).[31] The truth is, after decades of origin-of-life research, no one has any testable, let alone probable, theory for how life could have started by chance.[32] Eugene Koonin writes: "The origin of life field is a failure—we still do not have even a plausible coherent model, let alone a validated scenario, for the emergence of life on Earth."[33]

Or, as synthetic chemist James Tour puts it, "Those who think scientists understand the issues of prebiotic chemistry are wholly misinformed. Nobody understands them. Maybe one day we will. But that day is far from today. It would be far more helpful (and hopeful) to expose students to the massive gaps in our understanding. They may find a firmer—and possibly a radically different—scientific theory. The basis upon which we as scientists are relying is so shaky that we must openly state the situation for what it is: it is a mystery."[34] So, avowed naturalists like Dawkins are left with a belief in "sheer luck."

31. John Lennox, *God's Undertaker: Has Science Buried God?* (Oxford: Lion Hudson, 2009), 127–29. The difficulty lies not so much in generating *a* chain of amino acids, but a *functional* chain. It's a little like emptying a bag of scrabble letters on the floor and hoping it forms a coherent sentence, only it's much, much harder.

32. An article in *Science* magazine calls for an end to the fanciful dreaming: "Speculation should be restricted to the development of experimentally testable hypotheses that address key questions and provide a focus for progress." The authors call for a "radical rethink" to look for new "driving forces." Leroy Cronin and Sara Walker, "Beyond Prebiotic Chemistry," *Science* 352, no. 6290 (June 3, 2016): 1174–75. Accessed online at http://science.sciencemag.org/content/352/6290/1174.full.

33. Eugene Koonin, *The Logic of Chance: The Nature and Origin of Biological Evolution* (Upper Saddle River, NJ: FT Press, 2011), 391.

34. James Tour, "Animadversions of a Synthetic Chemist." Accessed online at http://inference-review.com/article/animadversions-of-a-synthetic-chemist.

The Origin of Complex Life: Evolution

Evolution is one of the cornerstones of Dawkins's argument against God. "I am a passionate Darwinian, believing that natural selection is, if not the only driving force in evolution, certainly the only known force capable of producing the illusion of purpose which so strikes all who contemplate nature."[35] In a world that undoubtedly looks designed, Dawkins must argue that the appearance of design is an illusion. Charles Darwin's theory of evolution for the first time gave atheists the supposed evidence of a mechanism that could produce such a world. However, even Dawkins cannot deny the appearance of purposeful design: "The illusion of purpose is so powerful that biologists themselves use the assumption of good design as a working tool."[36] "Biology is the study of complicated things that give the appearance of having been designed for a purpose."[37] While admitting apparent design, Dawkins leans heavily on evolution as a means to combat the argument of design, because it is a recent and (in his opinion) powerful rebuttal.

Definitions

In order to invoke evolution, we need to know what it is. Whenever someone asks me what I think about evolution, my response is always the same: "What do you mean by evolution?" Evolution is one of those slippery words that can be used in different ways to mean different things. If we are not all using words the same way, no consensus is possible. Here are a few ways the word can be used (or misused):[38]

35. Richard Dawkins, *A Devil's Chaplain: Reflections on Hope, Lies, Science, and Love* (New York: Mariner Books, 2003), 10.

36. Richard Dawkins, *River out of Eden: A Darwinian View of Life* (New York: Basic Books, 1995), 98.

37. Richard Dawkins, *The Blind Watchmaker* (New York: W. W. Norton, 1986), 1.

38. For further exposition, see Lennox, *God's Undertaker*, chap. 6.

1. Evolution = change over time (gradualism). This is a fairly uncontroversial and colloquial usage. We might describe the evolution of the mobile phone or an evolving story line. It is simply recognition of our changing reality. The word can be used to describe our natural world as well. We might talk about the evolving planet or an evolving mountain range, which simply means that the world today is not the same as it was yesterday.

2. Evolution = microevolution. This has a slightly narrower definition, but has still been observed and can be verified by anyone. Small changes in finch beak size are a good example of this. One way of putting this might be "change within limitations." Microevolution refers to variation in a living organism due to natural selection, mutation, changes in gene expression, and genetic drift. In other words, populations or individual families change over time, and some of those changes are noticeable and transmitted genetically. Bird beaks may change size and shape, but there are limits: a beak cannot change into a claw.[39] Notice that this type of change does not specify directionality. That is, change can be positive, negative, or neutral. For example, during a dry spell, finch beak lengths may shift to accommodate the harder nuts, but when the rain returns, the beak lengths may revert to the original length.[40] "The great majority of evolutionary changes at the molecular level . . . are caused not by Darwinian selection but by random drift of selectively neutral or nearly neutral mutations."[41]

39. For more on evolutionary limits, see Michael Behe, *The Edge of Evolution: The Search for the Limits of Darwinism* (New York: Free Press, 2007).

40. For a more complete handling of the Finch beak example, see Jonathan Wells, *Icons of Evolution* (Washington, DC: Regnery, 2000), chap. 8.

41. Motoo Kimura, *The Neutral Theory of Molecular Evolution* (Cambridge: Cambridge University Press, 1983), xi.

3. Evolution = macroevolution. For Dawkins, this is the most common usage of the word "evolution." It could be defined as change without limitations. If we extrapolate from micro-evolution, what prevents these changes that we do see, over exceptionally long periods of time, from producing new proteins, new structures, and even new organisms?[42] Therein lies the big question: can microevolutionary processes create anything *new*, or do they just rearrange things within existing limits? Is the extrapolation warranted?

Homology and Fossils

We run into problems immediately when we approach the issues of homology and the fossil record.[43] Homology is another way of saying similarity. So why are animals similar in either their body construction or their genetic makeup? Why is human DNA so close to chimpanzee DNA and so different from fish DNA? It could be because we share a closer common ancestor with chimps—*or* it could be because we share a more common bodily design with chimps.

Imagine you and I meet at a conference one day, and I surprise you by telling you that we have the same great-grandfather. Upon further inquiry, we find that this so-called shared relative is not alive, there is no testimony to his existence, and no records can be found. "But," I say, "our DNA is very similar!" Well, that might be because we are both human. Does similar DNA imply common ancestry or common function? Two animals with arms are going to need more similar instructions compared to animals without arms, so we would expect their DNA to look similar.

42. For further clarification on the different possible definitions of evolution, see Lennox, *God's Undertaker*, 100–103.

43. For an excellent primer on the subject, read Stephen Meyer, *Darwin's Doubt: The Explosive Origin of Animal Life and the Case for Intelligent Design* (New York: HarperOne, 2014).

That does not necessarily mean they have a common ancestor. For instance, instruction manuals for a bookcase and a desk will share certain similarities and be very different from the instruction manual for a computer. This is because the parts and purposes are similar, not because they share a common ancestor. So this is not evidence that supports evolution to the exclusion of other hypotheses. Conservation of form (or the DNA code for that form) may simply be reiteration of good design.

Dawkins posits thirty-nine rendezvous points for common ancestors (concestors) where the human line splits off from other major animal groups.[44] Yet there is no evidence for these concestors. Not one has been found. Not one is alive, and not one fossil remnant exists of any of these supposed concestors.

The Power of Chance

Let us now examine the heart of Dawkins's argument: evolution by natural selection occurs, and it is powerful enough to create all the complexity of this improbable world.[45] As Dawkins puts it, "Darwinian evolution uniquely solves the problem of life's statistical improbability, because it works cumulatively and gradually. It really does broker a legitimate traverse from primordial simplicity to eventual complexity—and it is the only known theory capable of doing so. Human engineers can make complex things by design, but the whole point is that human engineers need to be explained too, and evolution by natural selection explains them at the same time as it explains the rest of life."[46] Actually, Dawkins is missing the point. We can reliably detect

44. Richard Dawkins, *Brief Candle in the Dark: My Life in Science* (London: Bantam, 2015), 165–66. See also Richard Dawkins and Yan Wong, *The Ancestor's Tale: A Pilgrimage to the Dawn of Evolution*, rev. ed. (New York: Mariner Books, 2016).

45. Dawkins describes natural selection as "the process which, as far as we know, is the only process ultimately capable of generating complexity out of simplicity" (*The God Delusion*, 180).

46. Dawkins, *Brief Candle in the Dark*, 420.

and identify complex engineering design without knowing any-thing about the engineer.[47] For example, you clearly know at a glance that the Statue of Liberty was designed, even if you do not know by whom. In this case, the identity of the designer is secondary to the question of design.

Regardless, we might say, "biological complexity is simply too complex. It is statistically impossible that it could arise by chance." Dawkins counters, "What's wrong with the argument from statistical improbability, of course, is that natural selection is not a theory of chance. Natural selection is the non-random filtering of random variation, and the reason it works is that the improvement is cumulative and gradual."[48] Dawkins explains further: "'Did all of this happen by chance? Or did it happen by intelligent design?' Once again, no of *course* it didn't happen by chance. Once again, intelligent design is not the proper alter-native to chance. Natural selection is not only a parsimonious, plausible and elegant solution; it is the only workable alternative to chance that has ever been suggested."[49]

So, Dawkins wants a third way—one that does not hinge on design, but also does not rely on chance. He himself acknowl-edges that chance is an unsatisfactory explanation.[50] However, natural selection can only work on "random variation"—in other words, "chance variation." Even if natural selection is not a chance process, it cannot accomplish anything without chance mutation. Therefore, chance is the rate-limiting step of evolution by natural selection.

For example, consider a series of three doors in a hall, each

47. For more on our intuitive ability to detect design, see Douglas Axe, *Undeniable: How Biology Confirms Our Intuition That Life Is Designed* (New York: HarperOne, 2016).

48. Dawkins, *Brief Candle in the Dark*, 417.

49. Dawkins, *The God Delusion*, 145.

50. "It is grindingly, creakingly, crashingly obvious that, if Darwinism were really a theory of chance, it couldn't work." Dawkins, *Climbing Mount Improbable*, 77.

door opening to the next, with a digital push-pad, combination lock next to each door. Once you have entered the proper code into the first lock, natural selection can "fix" that code in place and hold the door open so a whole population can pass through and work on the second door. Clearly, the most time-consuming part here is the random sampling of combinations to find the correct code. Genetic mutations are like a random sampling of combination codes. What we are saying is that the number of doors and the number of digits necessary for the correct combination on each door are so large as to make it simply impossible to randomly achieve life in our world. Natural selection has to sit and wait impossibly long for random mutation to open each door. Empirical calculations estimate that, in the history of the universe, random mutation has only had time to attempt one ten trillion, trillion, trillionth of the possible combinations for a single door, out of thousands of doors.[51]

The Power (and Weakness) of Natural Selection

Dawkins tries to support macroevolutionary theory with evidence, but this is where it gets messy. You will notice that only the third definition of evolution mentioned above is controversial, yet Dawkins will frequently fail to distinguish which kind of evolution his interpretation of the evidence supports. Perhaps an example will be helpful:

> Selection—in the form of artificial selection by human breeders—can turn a pye-dog into a Pekinese . . . in a few centuries. The difference between any two breeds of dog gives us a rough idea of the quantity of evolutionary change that can be achieved in less than a millennium. . . . How many millennia do we have available to us in accounting for the whole history of life? . . .

51. Meyer, *Darwin's Doubt*, 201–8.

The time that has elapsed since our fish ancestors crawled out of the water on to the land is about twenty thousand times as long as it took to make all the different . . . breeds of dogs from the common ancestor that they all share. . . . It becomes rather easy to accept that evolution could accomplish the amount of change that it took to transform a fish into a human.[52]

In this passage, Dawkins conflates micro- and macroevolution. For him, microevolution *is* macroevolution, just on a smaller scale. But is that really true? Are there limits to evolution? Are there actually any differences between micro- and macroevolution? Is there a boundary point past which change is not possible without intentional intervention? Or, are we just continually moving the goalposts, saying, "OK, well now you have shown us *this* kind of change, but we still have not seen *that* kind of change"? In point of fact, there is a delimiting point that separates micro- and macro-evolution: alteration versus innovation.

Let us use Dawkins's example of dog breeding. Ignoring for the moment the fact that artificial selection is a carefully controlled and intelligently designed breeding process that accelerates change at speeds beyond anything we see in the natural world, is anything new at the molecular level being created, or are we just shuffling around what is already there in the genetic code? Although differences in dogs may appear quite significant on the surface, is anything *new* being made—or is there just variation in what already exists? It is frequently difficult to distinguish which is which until we look at the level of genes and molecules. In terms of dogs, as far we know, when we examine the genetic makeup, no true informational innovations have occurred. Let us examine this issue in more depth.

52. Richard Dawkins, *The Greatest Show on Earth* (New York: Free Press, 2009), 81–82.

How powerful is the power of natural selection? Can natural selection actually generate complexity? I referenced Dawkins's compelling story in chapter 2, but it is worth examining more closely: "One side of the mountain is a sheer cliff, impossible to climb, but on the other side is a gentle slope to the summit. On the summit sits a complex device such as an eye or a bacterial flagellar motor. The absurd notion that such complexity could spontaneously self-assemble is symbolized by leaping from the foot of the cliff to the top in one bound. Evolution, by contrast, goes around the back of the mountain and creeps up the gentle slope to the summit: easy!"[53]

Notice here that Dawkins is telling a story, a story with a lot of assumptions and no real justification for those assumptions. It could very well be a fairy tale. This story assumes that a gentle slope to the top of the complex device exists. Biologically speaking, this is a huge assumption. No such slope has ever been seen, shown, or even reasonably described. To borrow Dawkins's own analogy, what we actually see in biology is examples of organisms moving up and down through the same five-foot elevation on the mountain. The imaginative stretch here is remarkable. It is akin to saying that because I can climb the first five feet of Everest, I can climb to the peak. Actually, it is more like saying that because I can climb a mountain, I can climb to the moon.

In fact, some biologists think they have found sections of unclimbable "mountain" that evolution would need to traverse en route to the summit. They call these sections "irreducibly complex."[54] They have examined a particular hill or mountain and cannot find any way to climb up it, because it has sheer cliffs all the way around it. No gradual path is possible. No gentle slope exists. Dawkins might simply retort that they just have not looked

53. Dawkins, *The God Delusion*, 147.
54. For a more technical presentation of this idea, see Michael Behe, *Darwin's Black Box: The Biochemical Challenge to Evolution* (New York: Free Press, 2006).

hard enough or that a path will eventually be found.[55] But when a team of scientists spends years and can't find a path, it should at least give us pause. It is true that just because something appears to be irreducibly complex, that does not mean it is, but at what point do we seriously reconsider this as an option? Unless you are shackled by naturalism, the conclusion could be irreducible complexity. Theoretically, a mountain could be sheer all the way around. Actually, it seems that many sheer mountains have been found, and this should make us slow down and rethink.

The Origin of Innovation

Beyond the problem of sheer versus gradual pathways, there is an even more significant issue with evolution by natural selection. In order for macroevolution to be true, natural selection, working on genetic mutation, needs to create, not just alter. It needs to be able to make something new. It needs to show that it can generate complexity. All the evidence for evolution is for microevolution: rearrangement of what is already present in the genetic pool; no new complexity.[56] Indeed, every example of evolution that Dawkins presents in *The Greatest Show on Earth* is evidence of microevolution: alteration without innovation.

An analogy might help with this. A group of Lego bricks can be rearranged, but can it create more Legos? Biologically, we are finding out a lot about the different possibilities within a set of Legos, but not ideas on how to generate new Legos. Five unique Lego pieces can be rearranged to make something "more complex," depending on your definition, but to extrapolate from

55. "Those people who leap from personal bafflement at a natural phenomenon straight to a hasty invocation of the supernatural are not better than the fools who see a conjuror bending a spoon and leap to the conclusion that it is 'paranormal'" (Dawkins, *The God Delusion*, 155).

56. For more on the failure of evolutionary theory to explain the origin of information in DNA, see Stephen Meyer, *Signature in the Cell: DNA and the Evidence for Intelligent Design* (New York: HarperOne, 2009).

that rearrangement and say that the same processes can generate seven Lego pieces is wishful thinking. You might be able to make something "new" by removing Lego pieces (deleting/harming genetic material—a frequent strategy in antibiotic resistance[57]), but destroying does not help with the problem of creating.[58] What if a friend gives you new Lego pieces?[59] Well, this still does not solve the problem, because now we need to know where he got his pieces, and, in addition, studies show that natural selection tends to throw away duplicate pieces.[60] Yet, evolutionists have a huge media celebration when someone finds a group of six Lego pieces: a transitional form! But as you can see, it is not an explanation for how those extra pieces came to be there in the first place. Natural selection has been observed to rearrange Lego pieces, but never create them. The existence of six Lego pieces provides no explanation for how one might go from five to six, something we have never seen happen in biology.

In reality, we have oversimplified the whole situation for the purpose of clarity. Anyone playing with Legos knows that you can take the whole thing apart and put it back together however you wish. Biologically, though, there are rules about how the Lego pieces can be altered. For example, every single alteration or change has to result in a functional Lego model. Biologically speaking, functionless models are discarded. As you can imagine, this would severely limit the kinds of variation that could

57. Alison K. Hottes, Peter L. Freddolino, Anupama Khare, Zachary N. Donnell, Julia C. Liu, and Saeed Tavazoie, "Bacterial Adaptation through Loss of Function," *PLoS Genetics* 9(7), July 2013, 1–13. Accessed online at https://www.ncbi.nlm.nih.gov/pmc/articles/PMC3708842/.

58. Marcia Stone, "For Microbes, Devolution Is Evolution," *BioScience* 64, no. 10 (October 2014): 956.

59. In biology, this is known as horizontal gene transfer.

60. For more on the problems of gene duplication, see Joseph Esfandiar and Hannon Bozorgmehr, "Is Gene Duplication a Viable Explanation for the Origination of Biological Information and Complexity?" *Complexity* 16, no. 6 (2011): 17–31.

occur. There are many ways to arrange five Lego pieces, but only a handful of configurations make something useful. The useless ones are not preserved and cannot be used as intermediates on the way to building a useful model. This is sometimes known as the "sampling" problem.[61]

Lennox sums it up nicely: "There is no publication in the scientific literature—in prestigious journals, specialty journals, or books—that describes how molecular evolution of any real, complex, biochemical system either did occur, or even might have occurred."[62] There are no known examples of creation without intelligent input. There is quite a bit of speculation, but no evidence.

In reality, scientists are stuck. They can use selective pressure and mutation to optimize what is already there, but cannot create. As Dan Tawfik of the Weizmann Institute in Israel says, "Once you have identified an enzyme that has some weak, promiscuous activity for your target reaction, it's fairly clear that, if you have mutations at random, you can select and improve this activity by several orders of magnitude. What we lack is a hypothesis for the earlier stages, where you don't have this spectrum of enzymatic activities, active sites and folds from which selection can identify starting points. Evolution has this catch-22: Nothing evolves unless it already exists."[63] Even the first step of generating an innovative protein fold in an existing protein (something which

---

61. For more on the sampling problem, see L. N. Spetner, "Natural Selection versus Gene Uniqueness," *Nature* 226 (1970): 948–49, and Douglas D. Axe, "The Case against a Darwinian Origin of Protein Folds," *BIO-Complexity* 1 (2010): 1–12.

62. Lennox, *God's Undertaker*, 124. The point was also conceded by Franklin Harold of Colorado State University: "[T]here are presently no detailed Darwinian accounts of the evolution of any biochemical or cellular system, only a variety of wishful speculations." Franklin M. Harold, *The Way of the Cell: Molecules, Organisms, and the Order of Life* (New York: Oxford University Press, 2001), 205.

63. Rajendrani Mukhopadhyay, "Close to a Miracle," *ASBMB Today* 12, no. 9 (October 2013): 12–13.

must have been done at least 1,200 times in history[64]) seems increasingly unlikely, if not impossible: "The results obtained here . . . suggest that the appearance of a completely new fold from an existing one is unlikely to occur by evolution through a route of folded intermediate sequences."[65]

Every so often someone claims to have discovered an innovative mutation or increase in complex information; however, all such findings so far, upon close inspection, have proved to be merely alterations of existing genetic material.[66] Dawkins himself spends a great deal of time discussing one such experiment by Richard Lenski, who tracked changes in a bacterial population over 45,000 generations (equivalent of approximately one million years in human generations).[67] And, according to Dawkins, what were the stunning results? "59 genes had changed their levels of expression,"[68] and one strain "suddenly acquired the ability to eat citrate."[69] Changing gene expression merely means changing the

64. According to current estimates by SCOP. Accessed online at http://scop.berkeley.edu/statistics/ver=2.06.

65. Francisco Blanco, Isabelle Angrand, and Luis Serrano, "Exploring the Conformational Properties of the Sequence Space between Two Proteins with Different Folds: An Experimental Study," *Journal of Molecular Biology* 285, no. 2 (January 1999): 741–53.

66. Christopher Hitchens references Jamie T. Bridgham, Sean M. Carroll, and Joseph W. Thornton, "Evolution of Hormone-Receptor Complexity by Molecular Exploitation," *Science* 32, no. 5770 (April 7, 2006): 97–101. Accessed online at http://science.sciencemag.org/content/312/5770/97. All that happened was that a protein was altered to make it bind more weakly. A protein that was thought to have developed new nylonase activity, turned out to have had previous, weak promiscuous nylonase activity. See K. Kato et al., "Amino Acid Alterations Essential for Increasing the Catalytic Activity of the Nylon-Oligomer-Degradation Enzyme of Favobacterium Sp," *European Journal of Biochemistry* 200, no. 1 (August 15, 1991): 165–69.

67. Zachary D. Blount, Christina Z. Borland, and Richard E. Lenski, "Historical Contingency and the Evolution of a Key Innovation in an Experimental Population of Escherichia coli," *Proceedings of the National Academy of Sciences of the United States of America* 105, no. 23 (June 2008): 7899–906.

68. Dawkins, *The Greatest Show on Earth*, 124.

69. Ibid., 127.

amounts of already existing proteins, but a new ability sounds like innovation. However, genetic analysis revealed that the bacteria already had the ability to eat citrate, but it was normally suppressed.[70] So, in the end, "no new genetic information (novel gene function) evolved."[71] Furthermore, many of the changes observed in Lenski's bacteria resulted from loss-of-function or decrease-in-function mutations, which is the exact opposite of complexity creation.[72] And so, after 45,000 generations, still nothing new.

The point is largely conceded in a recent publication by the Royal Society:

> A rising number of publications argue for a major revision or even a replacement of the standard theory of evolution [2–14], indicating that this cannot be dismissed as a minority view but rather is a widespread feeling among scientists and philosophers alike. . . . For instance, the theory largely avoids the question of how the complex organizations of organismal structure, physiology, development or behavior—whose variation it describes—actually arise in evolution. . . . The real issue is that genetic evolution alone has been found insufficient for an adequate causal explanation of all forms of phenotypic complexity, not only of something vaguely termed "macroevolution."[73]

70. Z. D. Blount, J. E. Barrick, C. J. Davidson, and R. E. Lenski, "Genomic Analysis of a Key Innovation in an Experimental Escherichia coli Population," *Nature* 489, no. 7417 (September 2012): 513–18.

71. D. J. Van Hofwegen, C. J. Hovde, and S. A. Minnich, "Rapid Evolution of Citrate Utilization by Escherichia coli by Direct Selection Requires citT and dctA," *Journal of Bacteriology* 198, no. 7 (February 2016): 1022–34.

72. M. J. Behe, "Experimental Evolution, Loss-of-Function Mutations, and the 'First Rule of Adaptive Evolution,'" *Quarterly Review of Biology* 85, no. 4 (December 2010): 419–45.

73. Gerd B. Müller, "Why an Extended Evolutionary Synthesis Is Necessary," *Interface Focus* 7 (2017): 20170015. Accessed online at http://rsfs.royalsociety publishing.org/content/royfocus/7/5/20170015.full.pdf.

In other words, the current theory cannot adequately explain origins and innovation.

Dawkins thinks that if we can find a way to satisfactorily explain the design of the world without referencing God, then God must not exist. We have here attempted to summarize some of the philosophical and scientific weaknesses of such a view. Our universe is not possible or coherent without God's sustaining hand.

8

THE QUESTION OF GOD

It is some encouragement that Dawkins is at least willing to acknowledge that a world without God would look very different from a world with him: "A universe in which we are alone except for other slowly evolved intelligences is a very different universe from one with an original guiding agent whose intelligent design is responsible for its very existence."[1] Christians have said all along that studying the world that God created without studying the Creator will never produce a full picture, like studying a new technology without talking to the inventor.

But even if Dawkins does acknowledge the possibility of God existing, it is important to clarify which "god" he is talking about. Dawkins says, "When asked whether I am an atheist, [I] point out that the questioner is also an atheist when considering Zeus, Apollo, Amon Ra, Mithras, Baal, Thor, Wotan, the Golden Calf and the Flying Spaghetti Monster. I just go one god further."[2] However, this is not a fair assessment, because none of

---

1. Richard Dawkins, *The God Delusion* (New York: Houghton Mifflin, 2006, 2008), 85. "A universe with a creative superintendent would be a very different kind of universe from one without" (78).

2. Ibid., 77.

these deities have made the claims that God has, nor is there any substantiating evidence for their existence. There is no testable evidence or testimony for the Flying Spaghetti Monster. But the God of Scripture himself claims to be the true and only God (Deut. 4:35; Isa. 45:5–6).

Dawkins contradicts himself by testifying that the Christian God, if real, would have a very tangible and visible impact on this world that none of those other deities claim to have. Evidence exists for God as recorded in Scripture. Dawkins asks, "Did Jesus have a human father, or was his mother a virgin at the time of his birth? . . . Did Jesus raise Lazarus from the dead? Did he himself come alive again, three days after being crucified? There is an answer to every such question, whether or not we can discover it in practice, and it is a strictly scientific answer."[3] While we would not agree with his strict naturalistic limitations, Dawkins does have a point. The resurrection of Jesus is said by Christians to have been a real historical event with more than five hundred witnesses, written accounts, and eyewitness martyrs. It either happened physically or it did not. Only in Christianity do we have a living Savior. Christians confess that if the resurrection of Christ did not happen, then our faith is utterly futile (1 Cor. 15:14).

So, who is this God that Dawkins denies? Do Dawkins and other atheists represent him fairly and accurately, or do they fashion a god of their own fancy to attack? Atheist Carl Sagan complains in his book *Pale Blue Dot*: "How is it that hardly any major religion has looked at science and concluded, 'This is better than we thought! The Universe is much bigger than our prophets said, grander, more subtle, more elegant'? Instead they say, 'No, no, no! My god is a little god, and I want him to stay that way.' A religion, old or new, that stressed the magnificence

3. Ibid., 82–83.

of the Universe as revealed by modern science might be able to draw forth reserves of reverence and awe hardly tapped by the conventional faiths."[4] Yet this is exactly the vision of the world and of God that we get from the Bible:

> Lift up your eyes on high and see:
>> who created these?
> He who brings out their host by number,
>> calling them all by name;
> by the greatness of his might
>> and because he is strong in power,
>> not one is missing. (Isa. 40:26)

> But ask the beasts, and they will teach you;
>> the birds of the heavens, and they will tell you;
> or the bushes of the earth, and they will teach you;
>> and the fish of the sea will declare to you.
> Who among all these does not know
>> that the hand of the LORD has done this?
> In his hand is the life of every living thing
>> and the breath of all mankind. (Job 12:7–10)

> By the word of the LORD the heavens were made,
>> and by the breath of his mouth all their host.
> He gathers the waters of the sea as a heap;
>> he puts the deeps in storehouses.

4. Carl Sagan, *Pale Blue Dot: A Vision of the Human Future in Space* (New York: Random House, 1994), 52. As Dawkins puts it, "The kinds of views of the universe which religious people have traditionally embraced have been puny, pathetic, and measly in comparison to the way the universe actually is. The universe presented by organized religions is a poky little medieval universe, and extremely limited" ("A Survival Machine," in *The Third Culture*, ed. John Brockman [New York: Simon & Schuster, 1996], 75–95).

Let all the earth fear the LORD;
   let all the inhabitants of the world stand in awe of him!
(Ps. 33:6–8)

O LORD my God, you are very great!
You are clothed with splendor and majesty,
   covering yourself with light as with a garment,
   stretching out the heavens like a tent.
. . . .
O LORD, how manifold are your works!
   In wisdom have you made them all;
   the earth is full of your creatures. (Ps. 104:1–2, 24)

The universe is bigger and grander than we ever imagined, and the Bible told us it would be so. As we shall see, it is actually Dawkins who wants to put God in a box and strip him down to human standards. This makes him a non-god or just a really "intelligent natural being, with a super-body and a super-brain."[5] Dawkins likes to create a god who looks a lot like a powerful man, or a version of himself, and then deconstruct that.[6]

Would God be God if we could fully understand him? Dawkins displays some presumption in assuming that if God exists, we would be able to perfectly and wholly understand him. On the contrary, the fact that there are some things we do not fully understand about God is actually an argument in favor of his existence.

God himself proclaims this in the Bible: "For my thoughts are not your thoughts, neither are your ways my ways, declares the LORD. For as the heavens are higher than the earth, so are

5. Thomas Nagel, "The Fear of Religion," *The New Republic*, October 23, 2006.
6. Francis Collins says, "Dawkins is a master of setting up a straw man, and then dismantling it with great relish" (*The Language of God: A Scientist Presents Evidence for Belief* [New York: Free Press, 2006], 164).

my ways higher than your ways and my thoughts than your thoughts" (Isa. 55:8–9).

If we could fully understand God, we would be God! As Van Til aptly says, "God has self-contained and man has derivative knowledge."[7] "Created man is unable to penetrate to the very bottom of this inherently clear revelation. But this does not mean that on this account the revelation of God is not clear, even for him. Created man may see clearly what is revealed clearly even if he cannot see exhaustively. Man does not need to know exhaustively in order to know truly and certainly."[8] Dawkins's adherence to naturalism by definition commits him to a confined, restricted view of God.

This is one of a series of fallacious arguments that Dawkins and others frequently make about God. We can call it the "If I were God" argument. They follow a general pattern that goes like this: "If I were God, or if God existed, then I/he would do/say/make/behave like X. Since X is not so, God does not exist." Upon closer inspection, we find that the initial dependent clause is almost always wrong. We see one example of this above: If God existed, he would be completely understandable and explainable. No, he would not. Now let us evaluate a few more examples of this argument that you may encounter.

If God Existed, There Would Not Be So Many Religions

Actually, the plurality of religions is itself evidence that one of them is true. We should expect counterfeits of truth. Many deviations, especially of a similar nature, point to one opposing truth. In fact, the Bible itself predicts the existence of counterfeit

7. Cornelius Van Til, *Christian Apologetics*, 2nd ed., ed. William Edgar (Phillipsburg, NJ: P&R Publishing, 1976, 2003), 32.

8. Ibid., 77.

religions (2 Peter 2:1; 1 John 4:1). The existence of belief in many gods does not disprove the existence of the one true God. When asked, "Why this one God?" we can respond with God's self-attestation in the Bible and other evidence.

If God Existed, the Efficacy of Prayer Would Be Scientifically Demonstrable

Dawkins describes at great length a scientific attempt to analyze prayer.[9] Unfortunately, no Christian would agree with the initial premise, so the experiment adds nothing to his argument. The God of the Bible is not a genie who bends to our every whim. God promises to answer prayers, but he can answer them any way he pleases, even by saying no. In order to test the effectiveness of prayer, we would have to know the mind and will of God, which we do not.

If God Existed, Human Souls Would Be Materially Identifiable and Testable

Stenger asserts: "In short, after over a century of unsuccessful attempts to find convincing scientific evidence for the almost universally desired immortal and immaterial soul, it seems very unlikely that it, and a God who provides us with such a gift, exists."[10] Here Stenger protests that since there is no material evidence for an immaterial soul, it must not exist and so God must not exist. All of Stenger's material testing was seeking something that does not materially exist. Something that is immaterial *should* fail material investigation. He misrepresents what the soul is and what we expect from it.

9. Dawkins, *The God Delusion*, 85–90. See also Victor Stenger, *God: The Failed Hypothesis* (Amherst, NY: Prometheus Books, 2007), chap. 2.
10. Stenger, *God: The Failed Hypothesis*, 105.

If God Existed, He Would Be Good

Stenger also asserts: "Indeed, the God of . . . Christianity . . . can hardly be called omnibenevolent—or even very benevolent. . . . The reader is invited to simply pick up an Old Testament, . . . open to a random page, and read for a while. It will not take you long to find an act or statement of God that you find inconsistent with your own concepts of what is good. And . . . much in the Gospel can hardly be called 'good.'"[11] Notice that Stenger defines benevolence to mean "good." Google actually defines it as "the quality of being well-meaning; kindness." It bears repeating: God is not a genie whose job it is to make us happy and comfortable. Notice what the standard for "good" is here. It is relative to a human individual. Each person might define "good" differently, according to their own views. The Bible actually states that our sense of good is twisted (Jer. 17:9), which is why we have God's absolute standard for comparison. "Good" may refer to justice, or loving discipline, or things that we do not understand. All of Stenger's examples (as well as Dawkins's), upon further investigation, actually have explanations in keeping with God's perfection. Stenger never shows that anything God does is not "good."

If God Existed, He Would Be Constantly Watching over People like a Tyrant or Big Brother, Always Judging, Controlling, and Condemning

This is more an appeal to fear (and freedom from accountability) than an actual argument. It is true that when imperfect people and governments have this kind of control, it is frequently

11. Ibid., 34. Dawkins similarly lambasts the God of the Old Testament as "jealous and proud of it; a petty, unjust, unforgiving control-freak; a vindictive, bloodthirsty ethnic cleanser; a misogynistic, homophobic, racist, infanticidal, genocidal, filicidal,

misused, with devastating results. We do not trust tyrants, dictators, or totalitarian governments for this reason. However, God is not just a bigger version of a human; he is supernatural. He is perfect, holy, and without sin. The Bible portrays him as Father, a shepherd, a healer, loving, merciful, and a protector. He is not just some parent who tries to love us, but makes mistakes. Because he is perfect, he knows us perfectly and actually *can* care for us perfectly. He does not make mistakes. That should evoke feelings of comfort, rather than fear, for those who are reconciled to him.

If God Existed, the Bible Would Have Been Written Differently

Ill-informed forays into theology seem to be standard fare for atheists. Stenger, Hitchens, and Dawkins all attempt textual criticism, but do so without consulting theologians or Bible scholars.[12] They misread the Bible, imposing their own interpretive lenses to draw conclusions that theologians disagree with. They impose modern standards of writing on a text that God caused to be written for all mankind, for all time, for both ancient Middle Eastern peoples and twenty-first-century scientists.

If God Existed, Religion Would Be Clear and without Error

"Religion is man-made. Even the men who made it cannot agree on what their prophets or redeemers or gurus actually said or did. . . . The person who is certain, and who claims divine

---

pestilential, megalomaniacal, sadomasochistic, capriciously malevolent bully" (*The God Delusion*, 51).

12. See Dawkins, *The God Delusion*, 117–23; Hitchens, *God Is Not Great*, chap. 7; Stenger, *God: The Failed Hypothesis*, chap. 5.

warrant for his certainty, belongs now to the infancy of our species."[13] On the contrary, religion is man-*involved*, and therefore we should expect flaws resulting from man's sinful nature. Even if we do not know everything perfectly, we believe in an omniscient God who does know all and who has revealed himself perfectly in his Word.

If God Existed, He Would Have Made Humans More Significant/Central

This is the argument from human insignificance: "The Earth is a very small stage in a vast cosmic arena. . . . Our posturings, our imagined self-importance, the delusion that we have some privileged position in the Universe, are challenged by this point of pale light. Our planet is a lonely speck in the great enveloping cosmic dark."[14] This argument assumes that size is everything. Why does smallness equal insignificance? In *The Privileged Planet*, Guillermo Gonzalez and Jay W. Richards actually make the argument that our size and location in space and time are incredibly well designed for us. Not only is it designed for our physical life, but also for our spiritual life, to enable us to maximally glorify God, which is the chief purpose of mankind.[15]

If God Existed, He Would Have Made the Universe Differently

According to Stenger, "If God created a universe with at least one major purpose being the development of human life, then it is reasonable to expect that the universe should be congenial to human life. If the universe were congenial to human life, then

13. Hitchens, *God Is Not Great*, 10–11.
14. Sagan, *Pale Blue Dot*, 7.
15. This is sometimes referred to as the "Goldilocks Enigma."

you would expect it to be easy for humanlike life to develop and survive throughout the universe."[16]

However, the premise of universal congeniality to human life is hardly self-evident. Stenger assumes that we know what God's plan for us would be, if God existed, which is that we should be happy and healthy. According to Scripture, however, God's purpose is that he be glorified. Making us comfortable is nowhere stated to be his particular goal. In fact, God declared that the fall would bring hardship to our lives (Gen. 3:17–19).[17] Nevertheless, by grace our planet and the whole universe is still congenial enough for us to live and thrive. Besides, who are to define "congenial" and say that it is not so?

Stenger states the argument another way: "The universe is not congenial to human life, being tremendously wasteful of time, space, and matter from the human perspective. It also fails to agree with the fact that the universe is mostly composed of particles in random motion, with complex structures such as galaxies forming less than 4 percent of the mass and less than one particle out of a billion."[18] The key here is "from the human perspective." But we are not talking about the human perspective! Our failure to see the use or purpose of the universe, does not mean there is none. Particle motion may seem random to us, but that does not mean it is. In our own limited and imperfect way, we have to try to consider things from God's perspective. This great expanse actually does serve a purpose, in that it makes us keenly aware of both our smallness and the magnitude of God (Ps. 19:1). The vastness also emphasizes how special we are, in that God cares enough about us to take on humanity for our sake.[19]

---

16. Stenger, *God: The Failed Hypothesis*, 154.

17. God in creation said that all was originally made good, but the fall into sin brought man and all creation into a groaning condition (Rom. 8:18–25).

18. Stenger, *God: The Failed Hypothesis*, 230.

19. The vast magnitude of God and his particular, intimate presence with us are

God has truly revealed his purposes in the Bible, but as his finite creations we should not expect to fully comprehend everything he does. God may accomplish his purposes with respect to creation and the universe in ways that are unexpected or do not make complete sense to us. This does not mean that God is lesser, but rather that we are limited and unable to fully comprehend or grasp the totality of God's plans (Rom. 9:20).

If God Existed, He Would Have Designed Organisms Better (the Argument from Bad Design)

The argument usually proceeds as follows: Organism X has a bad, inefficient, or poor design. If God were a good designer, he would have made it differently. Or, the argument is: Structure Y has no purpose. A good designer would not create something with no purpose or with a suboptimal purpose. For example:

> The anatomy of the human eye, in fact, shows anything but "intelligence" in its design. It is built upside down and backwards, requiring photons of light to travel through the cornea, lens, aqueous fluid, blood vessels, ganglion cells, amacrine cells, horizontal cells, and bipolar cells before they reach the light-sensitive rods and cones that transduce the light signal into neural impulses—which are then sent to the visual cortex at the back of the brain for processing into meaningful patterns. For optimal vision, why would an intelligent designer have built an eye upside down and backwards?[20]

These statements spring from the assumption that we have already discovered what is optimal, useful, and maximal. The

---

referred to as his transcendence and immanence, respectively.

20. Michael Shermer, *Why Darwin Matters: The Case against Intelligent Design* (New York: Holt, 2006), 17.

truth is, more and more of these arguments are falling apart. In the case of the eye, research has shown that an inverted human eye is actually quite good and probably advantageous compared to a "verted" eye.[21] Dawkins cites not only the inverted eye,[22] but also the recurrent laryngeal nerve as an example;[23] however, the nerve's "poor design" has since been disproven.[24] Increasingly, these supposed cases of purposelessness are falling to the wayside as we discover heretofore unknown functions with genius engineering solutions. The human appendix and so-called junk DNA are two other examples. The argument from bad design is beginning to look more like an argument from gaps, and those gaps are steadily disappearing.

In the next several chapters, we will focus on two special kinds of "If God existed" arguments: those related to miracles and morality.

21. A. M. Labin, S. K. Safuri, E. N. Ribak, and I. Perlman, "Müller Cells Separate between Wavelengths to Improve Day Vision with Minimal Effect upon Night Vision," *Nature Communications* 5 (July 8, 2014): 4319. See also John Hewitt, "Fiber Optic Light Pipes in the Retina Do Much More Than Simple Image Transfer," at https://phys.org/news/2014-07-fiber-optic-pipes-retina-simple.html; Alberto Wirth, Giuliano Cavallacci, and Federica Genovesi-Ebert, "The Advantages of an Inverted Retina: A Physiological Approach to a Teleological Question," *Developments in Ophthalmology* 9 (1984): 20–28; Jerry Bergman, "Inverted Human Eye a Poor Design?" at http://www.asa3.org/ASA/PSCF/2000/PSCF3-00Bergman.html.

22. Richard Dawkins, *The Greatest Show on Earth* (New York: Free Press, 2009), 353–55.

23. Ibid., 356–64.

24. Wolf-Ekkehard Lönnig, "The Laryngeal Nerve of the Giraffe: Does It Prove Evolution?" (September 2010). Accessed online at http://www.weloennig.de/LaryngealNerve.pdf.

9

THE QUESTION OF MIRACLES

If God Existed, Miracles Would Destroy Science

John Haught sums up the argument this way: "If physical laws are to be perfectly steady and free of caprice, then there can be no personal deity that can conceivably act or intervene in the natural world. . . . If the universe were open to unpredictable divine actions, miracles, or responses to our prayers, this would put limits on, and even undermine, the predictive power of science."[1] Dawkins is even more forthright: "Any belief in miracles is flat contradictory not just to the facts of science but to the spirit of science."[2]

Before we begin discussing this, it is important that we understand what a miracle is. Dawkins tends to define miracles as "a violation of God's own laws." Dawkins insists that if God exists, then "the reality we inhabit also contains a supernatural agent who designed the universe and . . . maintains it and even

1. John F. Haught, *God and the New Atheism* (Louisville: Westminster John Knox, 2008), 80–81.
2. David Van Biema, "God vs. Science," *Time*, November 5, 2006. Accessed online at http://content.time.com/time/magazine/article/0,9171,1555132,00.html.

intervenes in it with miracles, which are temporary violations of his own otherwise grandly immutable laws."[3] David Hume contends further:

> A miracle is a violation of the laws of nature; and as a firm and unalterable experience has established these laws, the proof against a miracle, from the very nature of the fact, is as entire as any argument from experience as can be imagined. . . . It is no miracle that a man, seemingly in good health, should die on a sudden: because such a kind of death, though more unusual than any other, has yet been frequently observed to happen. But it is a miracle that a dead man should come to life; because that has never been observed, in any age or country. There must, therefore, be a uniform experience against every miraculous event; otherwise the event would not merit that appellation.[4]

This may sound like a compelling and concerning objection, but there are several critical flaws in the assumptions of this argument. First, Dawkins assumes a capricious god would meddle in and overthrow the regularities necessary for science, making it impossible. But what if God promised otherwise? What if it is God himself who upholds and maintains the regularities that make science possible in the first place? "God is both free (thus demanding experiment) and unchangeable in his character (demanding rational reflection on our part)."[5] We have touched

3. Richard Dawkins, *The God Delusion* (New York: Houghton Mifflin, 2006, 2008), 82. Victor Stenger describes miracles in this way: "God steps in whenever he wishes to change the course of events, which may include violating his own laws as, for example, in response to human entreaties" (*God: The Failed Hypothesis* [Amherst, NY: Prometheus Books, 2007], 42).

4. David Hume, *An Enquiry concerning Human Understanding* (Indianapolis: Hackett Publishing, 1993), 10.1, 76–77.

5. Vern Poythress, *Redeeming Science: A God-Centered Approach* (Wheaton, IL: Crossway Books, 2006), 76.

on this before. There is no particular reason that this universe should be rational, orderly, and regular, aside from a God who makes it so (Gen 8:22).

As John Lennox points out, it is "only belief in a Creator that gives us a satisfactory ground for believing in the uniformity of nature in the first place."[6] Our experience is not necessarily truth. We may only have experienced uniformity, but that does not make it universally true. And, even if it is universally true, why is it so? What makes it so? What holds it all together uniformly?[7]

More critically, however, Dawkins has incorrectly defined miracles. A violation of God's laws would be of concern, because then it might imply that those laws are not omnipotent. Fortunately, a miracle is not a violation of the laws of nature; instead, it is a violation of our *expectation* of the laws of nature. Dawkins's definition implies that humans have a full and complete grasp of the real laws of nature: the exact words of God. Our knowledge of God (and how much he is above and beyond us) as well as our knowledge of ourselves and our limitations, should immediately make us suspect such a claim.[8]

For example, Newton's laws of mechanics have served us well and have helped many physicists and engineers through the decades; however, with Einstein and relativity, we discovered that Newton's laws were only very good approximations of reality at low velocities. Why should it surprise us that our ideas of "laws" are really just very good approximations of God's reality?

Therefore, when something surprises us, and violates one

---

6. John Lennox, *God's Undertaker: Has Science Buried God?* (Oxford: Lion Hudson, 2009), 205.

7. For further refutation of Hume's argument see John Earman, *Hume's Abject Failure: The Argument Against Miracles* (New York: Oxford University Press), 2000.

8. We shouldn't think of God in the same way a baby would think about Albert Einstein. We are categorically different. It's more like the way a worm would think about a human, although even this falls short (Isa. 55:8–9).

of *our* "laws," it does not mean that it has violated one of *the* laws—that is—God's spoken word of truth. Remember, we are not God. Scientific laws are our close guess at God's law. Herman Bavinck describes it beautifully: "For that reason a miracle is not a violation of natural law and no intervention in the natural order. From God's side it is an act that does not more immediately and directly have God as its cause than any ordinary event, and in the counsel of God and the plan of the world it occupies as much an equally well-ordered and harmonious place as any natural phenomenon."[9] God holds all things together. That means every single particle. Nothing is outside of his control. "All things were made through him, and without him was not any thing made that was made" (John 1:3).[10]

What God does in the universe does not disrupt or invalidate the work of science. God can use secondary causes at times and places that fit our everyday experience, or he can work outside of that. Vern Poythress explains:

> The word of God governs the regularities of the seasons, and of night and day. But it also governs the exceptional cases, where God may deviate from a hitherto observed regularity. . . . The deviation is just as rational as the rationality of his continuing to govern the world in a regular way most of the time. All the works of God harmonize rationally into a unified plan for the entire world, and for the entirety of history. . . . How his entire plan harmonizes is up to him. In many cases it may mean that the same regularities that the scientist observes apply to unusual

9. Herman Bavinck, *In the Beginning: Foundations of Creation Theology* (Grand Rapids: Baker, 1999), 250.

10. Abraham Kuyper writes: "There is not a square inch in the whole domain of our human existence over which Christ, who is Sovereign over *all*, does not cry: Mine!" (*Abraham Kuyper: A Centennial Reader*, ed. James D. Bratt [Grand Rapids: Eerdmans, 1998], 488, italics original).

events as well. The arrow that struck Ahab may have flawlessly obeyed the usual laws of mechanics and aerodynamics.[11]

What appears as chance to humans is really under God's sovereign control (Prov. 16:33).[12]

A pertinent example of how misguided human impressions and assumptions can affect our view of God comes from the watchmaker analogy. The analogy originated with William Paley, who used a watch in his argument for design:

> In crossing a heath, suppose I pitched my foot against a stone, and were asked how the stone came to be there; I might possibly answer, that . . . it had lain there forever: nor would it perhaps be very easy to show the absurdity of this answer. But suppose I had found a watch upon the ground, and it should be inquired how the watch happened to be in that place; I should hardly think of the answer which I had before given, that for anything I knew the watch had always been there. . . . The watch must have had a maker: there must have existed . . . an artificer . . . who formed it for the purpose which we find it actually to answer; who comprehended its construction and designed its use. . . . Every indication of contrivance, every manifestation of design, which existed in the watch, exists in the works of nature; with the difference, on the side of nature, of being greater or more, and that in a degree which exceeds all computation.[13]

11. Poythress, *Redeeming Science*, 180. An opposing soldier seemingly drew his bow at random (1 Kings 22:34), but God ordained that it hit Ahab (22:17, 23).

12. For more detailed discussion on miracles and chance, see C. S. Lewis, *Miracles* (1947; New York: HarperCollins, 1996), or Vern Poythress, *Chance and the Sovereignty of God: A God-Centered Approach to Probability and Random Events* (Wheaton, IL: Crossway, 2014).

13. William Paley, *Natural Theology; or Evidences of the Existence and Attributes of the Deity*, 18th ed. (Edinburgh: James Sawers, 1818), 12–14.

Dawkins jumps on this passage in *The Blind Watchmaker* in an attempt to show the power of natural selection to create things that look designed:

> All appearances to the contrary, the only watchmaker in nature is the blind forces of physics, albeit deployed in a very special way. A true watchmaker has foresight: he designs his cogs and springs, and plans their interconnections, with a future purpose in his mind's eye. Natural selection, the blind, unconscious, automatic process which Darwin discovered, and which we now know is the explanation for the existence and apparently purposeful form of all life, has no purpose in mind. It has no vision, no foresight, no sight at all. If it can be said to play the role of watchmaker in nature, it is the blind watchmaker.[14]

Dawkins's analogy fails, since natural selection has no foresight and a blind watchmaker is still a purposeful designer with foresight, planning, and purpose in mind, but the real point is to show again how individuals make unwarranted assumptions about God. Notice, for example, a watchmaker is a human with a human intellect making a human object with human purpose and design in mind. God is none of this. For example, if I were to ask you what makes an ideal watch, you might say that it needs to be accurate, to never need a battery change, and to look super stylish. Notice how we impose human values and criteria on this designed watch. What we value and to what degree we value things will differ from person to person. What if the watch needed constant attention from the watchmaker in order to keep it from falling apart? We might think that the mark of a genius watchmaker would be his lack of involvement after creation, but is that necessarily so?

14. Richard Dawkins, *The Blind Watchmaker* (New York: W. W. Norton, 1986), 5.

What if God created a world that is completely and utterly dependent on him, where he has to be intimately involved in upholding and sustaining every particle every second? Does that mean he has created an imperfect world, or does it mean that he has made a world that he wants to be involved in? The world is contingent on him because he wants it to be. He delights in his creation and loves his creatures. This is not an argument for a watchmaker analogy, but merely a demonstration of how we and Dawkins have to be careful about imposing our Western ideas and presuppositions on God where they may not apply. In a conversation with someone like Dawkins, we should encourage a proper view of God and correct misconceptions, thus leading them to an admiration and love of the true God.

10

THE QUESTION OF EVIL

If God Existed, His Followers Would Be Better People and the World Would Be Better Than It Is

Dawkins and other atheists use different phrasing to say the same thing: because atheists sometimes do good and theists sometimes commit evil deeds, morals do not come from God and there is no God. He is saying, "Because good and evil don't look like what I would expect, if I were God, then God must not exist." There are various permutations of the argument, but essentially the call is to explain why Christians do bad things and atheists do good things. This view has been stated, perhaps most provocatively, by Weinberg: "Religion is an insult to human dignity. With or without it you would have good people doing good things and evil people doing evil things. But for good people to do evil things, that takes religion."[1]

As we have seen previously, definitions matter. The very definitions of "good" and "evil" are not easily agreed upon (or

1. Statement by Steven Weinberg at the Science Network's symposium "Beyond Belief: Science, Religion, Reason, and Survival," held at La Jolla, CA, November 5, 2006.

justified). For the moment, we shall examine some of the assumptions that are inherent in these premises.

Everyone Who Invokes Christianity Is a Christian

This is one of the more logically egregious assumptions. Although I might tell you that I am a 250-pound professional football player, one look at me would convince you otherwise. Claiming to be something does not make it true. Similarly, not everyone who claims to be a Christian is actually a Christian. Now this gets a little tricky, since we do not know and cannot judge the heart of a person, but it should at least give us pause when someone claiming to be a Christian does something that goes directly against the teaching of Christ. For example, it is hard to imagine how a true follower of Christ can justify beating his wife, given that the Bible explicitly commands husbands to "love their wives as their own bodies" (Eph. 5:28).[2]

Doing Something Bad in the Name of Christianity Invalidates All of Christianity

This is a corollary to the previous point. Lennox states it this way: "For, although the New Atheists' charge against Christendom for its violence may well be justified, their charge is not valid against the teaching of Christ himself. . . . Christendom is not the same as Christianity. . . . Christendom's violence was not Christian, for the simple reason that it was diametrically opposed to what Christ himself taught. . . . Following Christ means obeying his commandments. And one of those commands was the explicit prohibition of the use of force to defend Christ or his message."[3]

---

2. For the full context, see Ephesians 5:28–33. Christians can be identified by the "fruit" of their actions (Matt. 7:15–21).

3. John Lennox, *Gunning for God: Why the New Atheists Are Missing the Target* (Oxford: Lion Hudson, 2011), 64.

Christianity Is Responsible for
Morally Repugnant Violence

This argument is related to the first, but different in emphasis. Whereas the first argument talked about individuals, this second one targets Christian belief and religious practice that flows from it. Stated another way, religion produces violence, and "these deformities . . . arose not in spite of his faith, but because of it."[4]

However, the problem lies not in Christianity itself, but in mistaken interpretations. Christianity can no more generate violence than can a gun, a pen, or science. Christianity is not an active thing. It makes no choices and generates nothing. People as followers and believers make, choose, and generate. And people are flawed and have a terrible history of misusing guns, pens, and science. The idea that Christianity commits violence is about as meaningful as saying that science committed the nuclear attacks on Japan to end World War II. People are the perpetrators here.[5]

But does Christianity provide a particularly fertile ground for violent people? Dawkins has argued that "there is a sense in which the moderate, nice religious people—nice Christians, nice Muslims—make the world safe for extremists."[6] In other words, religion is a haven for violent people. It is true that horrors have been committed in the name of Christianity, but misuse of Christian doctrine does not nullify Christianity as a whole.

---

4. Christopher Hitchens, *God Is Not Great: How Religion Poisons Everything* (New York: Twelve Books, 2007), 187.

5. The Latin phrase *abusus non tollit usum* applies here, as it did in chapter 6: "abuse does not preclude proper use."

6. Hannah Furness, "Richard Dawkins: Churchgoers Enable Fundamentalists by Being 'Nice,'" *The Telegraph*, August 13, 2014. Accessed online at http://www.telegraph.co.uk/news/religion/11032654/Richard-Dawkins-Churchgoers-enable-fundamentalists-by-being-nice.html.

So, where does all this violence come from? Why do people do bad things in the name of Christianity? Where does this evil originate? If it is not Christianity itself, does religious fervor somehow trigger people to switch into a more evil state? Christianity actually has a compelling explanation. At the core, man is deeply broken. "For all have sinned and fall short of the glory of God" (Rom. 3:23). "As it is written: 'None is righteous, no, not one'" (Rom. 3:10). This means that people are born sinful and selfish.[7]

People may seek a belief, religion, faith, or worldview to match what they have already decided they want. Religion as a system can be a conduit for what is already there: sin. People can twist anything to serve their needs and desires. Moderate atheism, for example, has been used to justify violent extremism: burning of churches, euthanasia, and forced sterilization.[8] Sin is an opportunist. It uses whatever happens to be popular and powerful.

Overthrowing Christianity or any religious system will not get rid of evil and suffering. Sinful people will just latch onto some replacement and form it to serve their own ends. "Get rid of religion, and conflict and violence will simply find other occasions for their emergence and other grounds for their justification."[9] Evil finds its way out of the human heart by any means. Christianity can be misused to justify evil, but that does not make it inherently evil (or wrong). Christianity is not bad. How people improperly twist it can be.

Perhaps a case study will be useful here. It does not take much soul-searching for an individual to see that he is primarily

7. Jesus still calls us to love those who sin against us (Matt. 5:44).

8. For more on this, see John West, *Darwin Day in America* (Wilmington, DE: ISI Books, 2007).

9. Alister McGrath, *Why God Won't Go Away* (Nashville: Thomas Nelson, 2010), 79.

motivated by selfishness. Even our kind acts have selfish ends: to feel good about ourselves, get others to like us, or maximize opportunities for a successful, comfortable life. People are not inherently good. There is always a need for police, law, and governance. There are, to my knowledge, zero examples in history of communities that remain "good" without law—atheist or otherwise.

Yet Dawkins remains unjustifiably optimistic: "Perhaps, I . . . am a Pollyanna to believe that people would remain good when unobserved and unpoliced by God."[10] Dawkins himself offers the counterevidence. He relates the story of the police in Montreal going on strike on October 17, 1969. Without law, the city fell apart. However, he argues that "the majority of the population of Montreal presumably believed in God. Why didn't the fear of God restrain them?"[11] We have already shown that although the majority may *claim* that they believe, that does not mean they are believers or act as such. Christians are not perfect and can still sin and be selfish.

Hitchens latches onto this selfish streak in humans: "Is it not further true that all religions down the ages have shown a keen interest in the amassment of material goods in the real world?"[12] Unfortunately for Hitchens, atheism falls prey to his own religious critique. Many atheists have shown a "keen interest" in amassing material wealth. In reality, what a winsome, truthful worldview Christianity offers us! Christianity not only diagnoses the problem correctly (sin), but offers a necessary solution (Jesus).

Christianity is not about power and wealth, although people can try to twist it to be so. Christianity is truly all about acting out of loving gratitude for the incalculable eternal "wealth" we

10. Richard Dawkins, *The God Delusion* (New York: Houghton Mifflin, 2006, 2008), 261.
11. Ibid., 261.
12. Hitchens, *God Is Not Great*, 158.

have been undeservedly gifted. This gift cannot be lost or stolen. We have nothing left in this world to gain. "To live is Christ, and to die is gain" (Phil. 1:21).[13] We have been given the most valuable thing there is, and we want everyone to share in the gift! It is not about accumulation of material goods or power, but about unending giving from an unquenchable, overflowing heart resting in Christ (Luke 6:38; 2 Cor. 9:7).

If Christianity Is True, Christians Will Be Perfect

Although not explicitly stated, the idea is that somehow if a person professing to be a Christian makes a mistake, it means Christianity is faulty. Christianity itself, however, denies any such claim (1 John 1:8). We fully acknowledge our sin and strive by God's grace to be imitators of Christ. "And when Jesus heard it, he said to them, 'Those who are well have no need of a physician, but those who are sick. I came not to call the righteous, but sinners'" (Mark 2:17). Indeed, the heart of the gospel is that all men are sinners who need a Savior.

If Christianity Is True, Unbelievers Are Unable to Be Moral

Dawkins says something similar to this in *The God Delusion*: "Many religious people find it hard to imagine how, without religion, one can be good, or would even want to be good."[14] Again, this is not actually a Christian belief. Christianity attests that we are all made in the image of God and therefore, no matter what we might claim to believe about God, we all carry his

13. "Indeed, I count everything as loss because of the surpassing worth of knowing Christ Jesus my Lord. For his sake I have suffered the loss of all things and count them as rubbish, in order that I may gain Christ" (Phil. 3:8).
14. Dawkins, *The God Delusion*, 241.

mark as image-bearers. This includes a soul and a conscience (Rom 7:18).

Also, what justification does an atheist have for calling any action "good"? We all know that a nonbeliever is capable of refraining from murder. Apart from God, however, can that same individual provide justification for his view that murder is wrong? God alone is good and can define what is good (Ps. 119:68).

Atheists Can Be as Good as Christians

Dawkins puts it this way: "The way people respond to . . . moral tests, and their inability to articulate their reasons, seems largely independent of their religious beliefs or lack of them."[15] "Most people pay lip service to the same broad liberal consensus of ethical principles."[16] As mentioned above, this shared moral consensus (i.e., conscience) is explained by our shared humanity and creation in God's image. "They show that the work of the law is written on their hearts, while their conscience also bears witness, and their conflicting thoughts accuse or even excuse them" (Rom. 2:15).[17] Notice here that atheists and individuals of other religious traditions may profess not to believe in the God of the Bible, but functionally their hearts acknowledge the moral standards laid down by God, although, as sinners, they warp these standards.[18]

---

15. Ibid., 255.

16. Ibid., 298.

17. See also Isa. 30:21.

18. Interestingly, contrary to Dawkins's assertion, new research may indicate differences in how professed religious beliefs affect moral judgments about people. Religious belief correlates with a higher view of human rights. See John H. Evans, "Does Science Undermine Human Rights?," *New Scientist*, August 3, 2016. Accessed online at https://www.newscientist.com/article/mg23130850-200-who-we-think -we-are-and-why-it-matters/.

The flip side of this argument is the challenge put forth by Hitchens: "Name an ethical statement or action, made or performed by a person of faith, that could not have been made or performed by a nonbeliever."[19] This argument is more along the lines of "What sets Christians apart?" Most importantly, the life of Jesus is unique and cannot be replicated. Furthermore, because Christians have already attained the most valuable things there are—forgiveness of sins, peace with God, new life in Christ, and a promise of eternal relationship with God in heaven—there is a propensity for Christian believers to give sacrificially. Christians are more likely to be generous, even when there is good reason not to be.[20] Donating a million dollars to charity when you are a billionaire does not constitute real loss. However, it is an incredibly rare occurrence for someone to voluntarily give up power and privilege. For example, after serving two terms as president of the United States, George Washington stepped away from that power and voluntarily gave up serving additional terms. Perhaps Christianity led him to treasure something more than power. This difference only scratches the surface, however, as the most significant difference is not in outward actions, but in the heart's attitude of love for, and worship of, God.

To counter Hitchens's question, it goes both ways. Since the atheists are convinced that religion is so bad, can they name a horrible thing that could not be done by a "nonbeliever"?

When an Atheist Does Something Wrong, It Is Not Because of His Atheist Beliefs

When it comes to the issue of morally reprehensible actions, Dawkins is reluctant to look in the mirror. Everything we do

19. Hitchens, *God Is Not Great*, 289.
20. Religious people are four times more likely to donate to charities. See http://www.philanthropyroundtable.org/almanac/statistics.

is motivated by our beliefs. Sometimes our actual (functional) beliefs differ from what we profess to believe, but nothing is ever done for "lack of believing anything." Therefore, those who do not believe in God are motivated by their own beliefs when they do something evil. They act that way, at least in part, because they believe there is no God watching. There is no accountability. There is total freedom. Stalin and many Communists, if not Hitler and many Nazis, had no fear of divine recompense or judgment. There was nothing to hold them back. "As far as we can tell, very few of those carrying out the horrors of the twentieth century worried overmuch that God was watching what they were doing."[21] Atheists do act out of their atheistic worldview. It might be enlightening to discuss with an atheist how their worldview impacts all facets of their life.

---

21. David Berlinski, *The Devil's Delusion: Atheism and Its Scientific Pretensions* (New York: Crown Forum, 2008), 26–27.

11

THE QUESTION OF MORALITY

Now that we have discussed some of the protestations filed against Christian belief, let us turn our attention to Dawkins's understanding and formulation of morals. The question is not whether you can "do good," but why can you and why will you "do good"? And how do we know what "good" is? We must decide what is good and find a way to justify that decision. Consider what we do when no one is looking or when no one can punish us. How do we make such decisions? We must decide whether "goodness" is a matter of performing (or not performing) particular actions or if the intentions of the mind and heart play a role.

Can people "do good" for the wrong reason? Some of the kindest, most caring people I know are atheists. Yet there is a distinct difference between non-Christians doing good things and non-Christians having a justification for doing those things apart from God. Though Dawkins may be a moral individual, does his belief system provide a justifiable foundation for his moral beliefs or is he smuggling in preordained, God-given consciences when defining morals?

Let us look first at how Dawkinsian thinkers define morality. Several attempts have been made.

Morality as Adaptation

"Morality, or more strictly our belief in morality, is merely an adaptation put in place to further our reproductive ends. Hence the basis of ethics does not lie in God's will. . . . In any important sense, ethics as we understand it is an illusion fobbed off on us by our genes to get us to co-operate."[1] According to this view, our moral views are just adaptive instincts to promote our genes. As a result, all actions would be for purely selfish survival.

In addition, any moral action that does not have a Darwinian explanation is considered to be a "misfiring." Dawkins cites examples like Good Samaritan urges or the act of adoption, which have no selective advantage.[2] "Universal love and the welfare of the species as a whole are concepts that simply do not make evolutionary sense."[3] If Dawkins is right, we must determine what is a misfiring and what is not. Yet there is no way to really know what gives us a selective advantage and what does not. Atheism itself could be a "misfiring." If it is only a matter of opinion, we can end up continually changing our opinions over what is a misfiring. It is impossible to prove this right or wrong, since what makes "evolutionary sense" depends on how we interpret the world, and that can and does change. Who is to know the truth? How is the truth known? This leads inexorably to skepticism, where there is no absolute truth.

If we assume Dawkins's position to be true, our moral urges

1. Michael Ruse and Edward O. Wilson, "Evolution and Ethics," *New Scientist* 108 (October 17, 1985): 50–52.

2. Richard Dawkins, *The God Delusion* (New York: Houghton Mifflin, 2006, 2008), 252–53.

3. Richard Dawkins, *The Selfish Gene* (Oxford: Oxford University Press, 1976), 2.

are not rules or absolutes as much as guidelines for survival. We are under no obligation or compulsion to behave adaptively. We can choose to resist our feelings. If something is a misfiring, we can choose to act differently.[4] These moral urges are supposed to be working on behalf of the genes in our body, not necessarily the organism as a whole. But, in that case, there is no guide to know which urge to follow and which to resist. "Even if our ethical instincts evolved by natural selection, we still have to explain why we are obliged to obey them here and now, especially since they may be evolutionary 'misfirings.'"[5] Dawkins says we should trust our instincts, but then gives us reason not to trust our instincts, since some instincts are misfirings! How can the brain get outside its own evolutionary box to make decisions? Evolution may make the brain adaptive, but not reasonable.[6] Could we really trust our imperfectly evolved brains to reason our way to morals?

Given this view, Dawkins struggles to define good and evil and explain their origins. Everything just is. In fact, there is no such thing as good and evil. Killing someone might be maladaptive or an evolutionary "misfiring," but that does not make it evil. Normal animal behavior includes hunting and killing, and we consider that adaptive! We might feel that something is wrong, but our feelings are being manipulated for our survival, so we cannot trust them. We might try to reason, but we do not have any grounds or standard to reason from. We cannot trust our reason when it is just conditioned for survival. Maybe our brains are just telling us something is wrong because it will go better for our genes if we behave as if it were wrong.

"But, if a person is nothing but his/her genes, and these genes control his/her moral behavior, how could s/he ever be blamed

4. Ibid., 200–201.
5. John F. Haught, *God and the New Atheism* (Louisville: Westminster John Knox, 2008), 73.
6. Ibid., 74.

for doing wrong, or praised for doing right?"[7] This view would make punishment and justice impossible, since all behavior is inevitable and free will does not exist.[8] However, our genes do not compel us. We do not need to obey our genes. Obeying them does not make us good, and disobeying them does not make us evil. Dawkins's assessments of good and evil are just contrived human interpretations of evolutionary direction at a particular cultural time. Evolutionarily speaking, a saint in this age may be considered a criminal a few years from now, or vice versa, depending on how cultural perception changes and how people interpret science.[9]

Even by Dawkins's standards, we might decide that something is better for one person's genes, but that does not necessarily make it good. It could be good for one person's genes to murder those who are physically weaker, but bad for the whole species if those murdered are intellectually stronger. We cannot really know if it is good or bad in the long term—we just have to speculate. "What natural selection favours is rules of thumb, which work in practice to promote the genes that built them."[10] At best, according to Darwinism, breaking a "moral" absolute is not good or evil; it is just disadvantageous or maladaptive.

Dawkins himself sums it up nicely: "In a universe of blind physical forces and genetic replication, some people are going to get hurt, other people are going to get lucky, and you won't find

---

7. John Lennox, *Gunning for God: Why the New Atheists Are Missing the Target* (Oxford: Lion Hudson, 2011), 108.

8. Without free will, there is no basis for the criminal justice system. K. Burns and A. Bechara, "Decision Making and Free Will: A Neuroscience Perspective," *Behavioral Sciences and the Law* 25, no. 2 (2007): 263–80. And yet, some atheists do believe that free will is an illusion: Sam Harris, *Free Will* (New York: Free Press, 2012), 5.

9. If we arbitrarily "make our own purpose," then we have no grounds outside of ourselves for condemning the purposes that others (including murderers and rapists) define for themselves.

10. Dawkins, *The God Delusion*, 252.

any rhyme or reason in it, nor any justice. The universe that we observe has precisely the properties we should expect if there is, at bottom, no design, no purpose, no evil, no good, nothing but pitiless indifference."[11]

Morality as Individual Relativism

People rarely subscribe to this kind of fatalism, however. The current trend is to define purpose, meaning, and morality endogenously—that is, to construct and define our meaning individually, by ourselves, from within ourselves.[12] However, is that construction of meaning comprehensively true? In other words, just imagining something does not make it true. Anyone can imagine meaning for life, but if they are wrong, they have merely created the equivalent of an inconsistent, drug-induced escapism that lasts a lifetime. They therefore live a "noble lie," believing it is better to construct a false and unjustifiable moral system than to live consistently in nihilism.[13] Although this may allow a person to function internally by suppressing the truth, it is untenable in the real world of relationships.

This becomes eminently clear when two individuals' meanings conflict with each other. For example, suppose someone decides his purpose in life is to reduce overpopulation through worldwide genocide. In the individual world of meaning we have created for ourselves, this could be wrong, but unless there is some external, authoritative word, we cannot justifiably tell the

11. Richard Dawkins, *River out of Eden: A Darwinian View of Life* (New York: Basic Books, 1995), 132–33.

12. David Speed, Thomas Coleman II, and Joseph Langston, "What Do You Mean, 'What Does It All Mean?' Atheism, Nonreligion, and Life Meaning," *SAGE Open* 8, no. 1 (January 2018): 1–13. See also Viktor Frankl, *Man's Search for Meaning* (Boston: Beacon Press, 2006).

13. Greg Epstein, *Good without God: What a Billion Nonreligious People Do Believe* (New York: HarperCollins, 2009), 70.

individual that the personal meaning he has created for himself is wrong. Actual meaning cannot be self-generated, but it can be God-given (Gen. 1:26–28; Isa. 43:7; Eph. 1:11).[14]

Morality as Group Relativism

Individuals may disagree, but what about groups? Related to individual moral relativism is group moral relativism, where consensus dictates morality. This can lead people to fear,[15] not because groups are immoral or perhaps amoral, but because they are opportunistic moralists. Morality can change at any point to benefit a group. There is no guarantee that morals will not change suddenly, even if they have not for a long time.[16] "Morals do not have to be absolute," says Dawkins.[17] If so, we are only "right" because of current social, political, cultural, and historical consensus.[18] But those current sensitivities can change, so how can we condemn Nazis, Communists, or other regimes? They were right by some popular consensus back then, depending on whom you asked.[19] In other words, what is advantageous for your genes may change over time. It is up to mankind to decide what is advantageous. What mankind decides depends on power and popularity, and those things are constantly changing.

Atheist Elizabeth Anderson demonstrates this in her own view of morality:

---

14. In fact, the message of Christianity is that your life is so valuable and God loves you so much, that he was willing to give up his own life for yours (John 3:16).

15. Gallup Poll, June 22, 2015. Accessed online at http://www.gallup.com /poll/183713/socialist-presidential-candidates-least-appealing.aspx.

16. Epstein, *Good without God*, 35–37.

17. Dawkins, *The God Delusion*, 265. See also Richard Dawkins, *Brief Candle in the Dark: My Life in Science* (London: Bantam, 2015), 430–31.

18. Haught, *God and the New Atheism*, 73.

19. In this view, Dawkins would only be "right" relative to himself. Other cultures, individuals, and times may evolve opposite values.

We each have moral authority with respect to one another. . . . Moral rules spring from our practices of reciprocal claim making, in which we work out together the kinds of considerations that count as reasons that all of us must heed, and thereby devise rules for living together peacefully and cooperatively, on a basis of mutual accountability. What of someone who refuses to accept such accountability? Doesn't this possibility vindicate [the] worry, that without some kind of higher authority external to humans, moral claims amount to nothing more than assertions of personal preference, backed up by power? No. We deal with people who refuse accountability by restraining and deterring their objectionable behavior.[20]

So, what happens when two "moral authorities" conflict? When the impala complains to the cheetah, who is right and who is wrong? Anderson proves the very point laid against her, and in fact contradicts herself, when you examine her final sentences. When two moral authorities conflict, the more powerful one wins: might makes right. By her own definition, morality is not fixed, but is determined by what groups have the power to deter "objectionable behavior" by declaring some to be in violation of the group "preference." In this view, everything is permitted (nothing is inherently right or wrong). Some things are just "restrained" or permitted by those who happen to be in power. In the end, Anderson admits, "If you find a train of reasoning that leads to the conclusion that everything . . . is permitted, this *is* a good reason for you to reject it. . . . So, if it is true that atheism entails that everything is permitted, this is a strong reason to reject atheism."[21]

Christians know that morals do not just come from ourselves

20. Elizabeth Anderson, "If God Is Dead, Is Everything Permitted?," in *The Portable Atheist*, ed. Christopher Hitchens (Philadelphia: Da Capo Press, 2007), 335.
21. Ibid. Accessed online at http://www.skeptic.ca/Biblical_Ethics.htm.

or from a consensus where the powerful and the majority decide. We know our sin and our need for an external standard! I do not trust a person (or a group of people) to be perfect or completely unselfish when it comes to deciding what is and is not moral. Dawkins would say that there are some things we can all agree on. Can he prove that we all agree?[22] Even if we do, agreement does not make something true. Majority opinions on morality have changed in the past. We cannot be certain that things we agree on now will not change later. If there *are* moral standards, couldn't that be a result of the God-given conscience we all share as a result of being created in his image?

Scripture proclaims God as constant and unchanging (Mal. 3:6; Heb. 13:8). Therefore, there exists in him a constant, absolute, perfect moral standard that we can rely on, even if we, as flawed humans, sometimes have trouble discerning it.

Morality as Consequentialism

According to Dawkins, "The morality of an action should be judged by its consequences."[23]

This view generally defines evil as perpetrating or allowing unnecessary suffering.[24] But there is no accepted authority to judge consequences or decide what is necessary or unnecessary suffering.[25] There is no justification for saying that suffering is evil

22. This may be more difficult than Dawkins imagines. Even the morality of murder in the form of infanticide is now debated in some places. Cleuci de Oliveira, "The Right to Kill," *Foreign Policy*, April 9, 2018. Accessed online at https://foreignpolicy.com/2018/04/09/the-right-to-kill-brazil-infanticide/.

23. Dawkins, *The God Delusion*, 266.

24. See Victor Stenger, *God: The Failed Hypothesis* (Amherst, NY: Prometheus Books, 2007), 222, and Dawkins, *The God Delusion*, 298.

25. Modern secular counseling methodology defines morals through the eyes of a detached "ideal observer" (Kathryn C. MacCluskie and R. Elliott Ingersoll, *Becoming a 21st Century Agency Counselor* [Belmont, CA: Brooks/Cole Counseling, 2001], 80). However, we can't imagine such an observer because we can't disentangle his

or bad, except that we might feel that suffering is evil or agree that it is bad.[26] Westerners often use feelings as a basis for judgment, but feelings change. In addition, consequences may feel bad, but, according to Dawkins and others, our feelings are not to be trusted on the matter, because feelings are just "adaptive reflexes."

Dawkins speaks glowingly[27] of Sam Harris's attempts to fabricate a scientific basis for morality, centered around the nebulous concept of "well-being," wherein "well-being" will correspond to some as yet undiscovered and undefined "brain state."[28] First of all, even if it were to exist, we will never be able to agree upon such a brain state, since each of us will value different brain conditions, based on the preexisting conditions and worldviews of our own brains! "That is, whatever we count as 'well-being' will be influenced by what sorts of things we value and what we think reality is like."[29] In other words, each brain will have a different definition of what a "well" brain would look like—a kind of individual moral relativism again.

But Harris proceeds undeterred. He declares, "We simply must stand somewhere. I am arguing that, in the moral sphere, it

---

views from our own nonideal perspective (John Lennox, *God's Undertaker: Has Science Buried God?* [Oxford: Lion Hudson, 2009], 33). If we could imagine such an individual, we could be him—thus claiming to be ideal ourselves. If we can imagine that he exists, but also acknowledge that we can't be him, then the only way we can know him is through his own self-revelation. Christians say that God is the "ideal observer" and has revealed himself in Scripture.

26. Actually, some cultures perceive suffering to be both necessary and helpful.

27. Richard Dawkins: "I was one of those who had unthinkingly bought into the hectoring myth that science can say nothing about morals. To my surprise, *The Moral Landscape* has changed all that for me" (quoted in Sam Harris, *The Moral Landscape: How Science Can Determine Human Values* [New York: Free Press, 2010], 1).

28. Harris does not discuss whether morality is based on the well-being of individuals, humans, organisms, earth, or the universe, or even how we might determine which of those is more valuable, although he does acknowledge that this determination is problematic (*The Moral Landscape*, 68).

29. Mitch Stokes, *How to Be an Atheist: Why Many Skeptics Aren't Skeptical Enough* (Wheaton, IL: Crossway, 2016), 185.

is safe to begin with the premise that it is good to avoid behaving in such a way as to produce the worst possible misery for everyone."[30] No explanation is provided for why we should begin with that premise.[31] No definition of misery is agreed upon,[32] and no reasoning is given for why misery is "bad" and happiness is "good," other than one's own feelings on the matter.[33]

Here Harris runs into what is commonly known as the "is/ought" problem.[34] That is, even if we were to define what "well-being" *is*, who is to say why we *ought* to pursue it or why we *ought* to value it. "We can certainly use science to say *how* we can maximize well-being, once we define well-being,"[35] although even this may be impossible.[36] Without God, there is no reason *why* we should maximize well-being in the first place, except for Harris

30. Harris, *The Moral Landscape*, 39.

31. "How do we know that the morally right act is, as Harris posits, the one that does the most to increase well-being, defined in terms of our conscious states of minds? Has science really revealed that? If it hasn't then the premise of Harris' all-we-need-is-science argument must have non-scientific origins" (Kwame Anthony Appiah, "Science Knows Best," *The New York Times*, October 1, 2010. Accessed online at http://www.nytimes.com/2010/10/03/books/review/Appiah-t.html).

32. In fact, certain types of misery are designed to help us learn and thus increase our long-term survivability. So, can misery sometimes be a "good"?

33. Harris's view has difficulty delineating any distinctions between human and animals. A cheetah killing an impala is a pretty miserable experience for the impala, but no one declares that as a moral evil.

34. Classically stated in David Hume, *A Treatise of Human Nature* (Oxford: Clarendon, 1978), 469. See also Stokes, *How to Be an Atheist*, 156.

35. P. Z. Myers, "Sam Harris v. Sean Carroll," *Pharyngula*, May 4, 2010. Accessed online at http://scienceblogs.com/pharyngula/2010/05/04/sam-harris-v-sean-carroll/.

36. "One of the problems with consequentialism in practice is that we cannot always determine whether the effects of an action will be bad or good" (Harris, *The Moral Landscape*, 67). It is impossible for us to accurately predict future well-being (or the loss of it) for an individual. For example, a severe period of depression could result in a strengthening and maturing response that reaps benefits for decades, or it could result in suicide. How can we predict when, in the moment, the "brain states" may be identical? Individuals have different life experiences and worldviews that will impact final outcomes in unmeasurable and unpredictable ways.

declaring it so![37] People generally pursue some vague sense of personal well-being, but what makes them obligated to do so? Why *must* we value well-being? Why would it be wrong not to pursue personal well-being? We cannot simply say that something is right because it feels right, because then we need to know why our feelings are like that. What makes our feelings right in this matter?[38]

Harris presents no argument to contradict this point. He merely proclaims that if the is/ought distinction cannot be bridged, then the consequences would be disastrous.[39] He cannot bring himself to be consistent with his stated worldview and accept the abhorrent results that would necessarily follow.[40] He is left with no recourse but to make an unwarranted philosophical leap and bypass the is/ought gap because facing it would be devastating for his argument.

So Harris starts with an unjustified assumption, that "well-being" is "good," when the very definition of "good" is in question.[41] He confesses, "We must smuggle in an 'unscientific prior' to justify any branch of science. If this isn't a problem for physics, why should it be a problem for a science of morality?"[42]

---

37. For more on this, see William Lane Craig's debate with Sam Harris at the University of Notre Dame, April 2011. Accessed online at http://www.reasonable faith.org/is-the-foundation-of-morality-natural-or-supernatural-the-craig-harris. Additional commentary can be found in Tom Gilson and Carson Weitnauer, eds., *True Reason: Confronting the Irrationality of the New Atheism* (Grand Rapids: Kregel Publications, 2014), 63, 68.

38. Consequentialism can take various forms. Greg Epstein, in *Good without God*, uses the idea of human flourishing (34) centered around dignity (91). Although he mentions the is/ought distinction (31), he has no response (he merely deflects) and thus is left saying we should value human flourishing simply because we all "feel" it to be good, but that is just individual moral relativism.

39. Harris, *The Moral Landscape*, 42.

40. Stokes, *How to Be an Atheist*, 197–98.

41. Harris, *The Moral Landscape*, 12.

42. Sam Harris, "Toward a Science of Morality," *The Huffington Post*, July 6, 2010. Accessed online at http://www.huffingtonpost.com/sam-harris/a-science-of-morality _b_567185.html.

Unfortunately, it *is* a problem for atheistic physics. Naturalism demands that science explain all, and physics must smuggle in a priori natural laws, constants, and assumptions. These laws are not necessary consequences of naturalism. They are merely assumed. Harris contends that these things must be assumed, else the scientific enterprise and reason itself are in doubt,[43] but he is mistaken. Science and reason do not collapse; only his flawed foundation, his worldview, collapses, because it fails to adequately support science and reason. The Christian God is a necessary and sufficient foundation. God does not require science to deduce itself. He provides the foundational "priors" that science needs in order to operate; no smuggling is necessary.

Solving the Moral Problem

Dawkins has not solved the problem. We experience suffering; we sense injustice; we feel that we have influence over these things and are affected by them. We have strong impressions of right and wrong, yet Dawkinsian thinking leaves us without answers:[44] "Real moral disputes can be ended in lots of ways: by voting, by decree, by fatigue of the disputants, by the force of example that changes social mores. But they can never really be resolved by finding the correct answers. There are none."[45]

As Lennox puts it, "Atheism has not got rid of the suffering and the evil. They are still there. Moreover, atheism's 'solution' to the problem of evil has got rid of something else—hope. Atheism is a hope-less faith. Indeed, by removing hope, atheism can be

43. Harris, *The Moral Landscape*, 201–2.

44. For more on moral realism and the failure of naturalism to account for universal morality, see Scott B. Rae, *Doing the Right Thing: Making Moral Choices in a World Full of Options* (Grand Rapids, MI: Zondervan, 2013), 48–56.

45. Alexander Rosenberg, *The Atheist's Guide to Reality: Enjoying Life without Illusions* (New York: W. W. Norton, 2011), 98.

seen to make the suffering much worse."[46] Atheist Bertrand
Russell proves this point by his own admission: "[Man's] hopes
and fears, his loves and his beliefs, are but the outcome of acci-
dental collocations of atoms. . . . All the labours of the ages, all
the devotion, all the inspiration, all the noonday brightness of
human genius, are destined to extinction in the vast death of
the solar system. . . . Only within the scaffolding of these truths,
only on the firm foundation of unyielding despair, can the soul's
habitation henceforth be safely built."[47]

However, Christians know the origin of suffering, and their
own sinful participation in it. They also have hope in God's
promise of a world without suffering, won for us by Christ's aton-
ing death and glorious resurrection (Rev. 21:1–4). The God of
the Bible loves us, created us with a purpose, and gives us moral
instruction to maximize human flourishing for the glory of God.
Thus we desire to share and explain the clear existence of our
glorious hope to the world.

46. Lennox, *Gunning for God*, 136.
47. Bertrand Russell, "A Free Man's Worship," in *Mysticism and Logic and Other Essays* (Charleston, SC: BiblioLife, 2010), 47–48.

12

WHERE THE FUTURE LIES

Based on what we know about Dawkins, what can we say about the future? Although we are finite, based on God's truth revealed in Scripture, there are some things we can say with confidence.

Science Will Continue

At its core, science is a search for truth. Since God is the author, creator, and sustainer of all truth, truth will always be there (John 14:6). Since we are created in the image of God, we will always desire the truth and will seek after it. Granted, sinful hearts may distort, misinterpret, or deny the truth, but that does not diminish its existence or undermine science as one (limited) means of pursuing truth. In creating us and the world, God created the possibility and ability to do science. None of what he upholds can vanish.

Religion Generally, and Christianity Specifically, Will Not Go Away

Despite what Dawkins might hope for, the truth of Christ and his people can never be stamped out, for even the rocks cry out (Luke 19:40)! In fact, historically, Christianity thrives in the face of opposition. People are born into this world religious. We are born with a heart attitude that seeks to align itself either with God or against him (Ps. 51:5). We are religious by our very nature, and that cannot be removed or extinguished.

Atheism Will Not Go Away until Jesus Returns

But for the grace of God, hearts in rebellion will latch on to any excuse for unbelief. This means that atheism, in some form or other, will always exist, because people will always want a reason to justify their unbelief. This breaks our hearts and moves us into loving conversations with them.

We Should Not Fear Philosophical Influences in Culture, Including Atheism

There is always something to worry about. Whether it is the economy, the next election, the weather, or the growing influence of an increasingly secular culture, atheism is one voice in the milieu. Yes, Dawkins and the naturalistic worldview he espouses may be particularly loud and scary, but there is nothing particularly special or new about the challenges that Christians face from unbelief. In the garden of Eden, Satan tempted Eve with unbelief (Gen. 3:1–5).

Dawkins is a lot like fireworks: He burns hot, fast, and bright. He makes a lot of noise. But then, inevitably, he will disappear, leaving only a trail of smoke to tarnish the atmosphere. Some fireworks linger longer than others. Some are quickly lost in the cacophony of other new, more brilliant bursts. The world is small, and our time here is short (Gen. 3:19). We strive to shine as brightly as we can through the power of Christ in a darkening world (Matt. 5:16). Yet we all pale and vanish in the face of the true light of heaven, who gives light to all men: unflickering, unwavering, eternal, sustaining, and satisfying to all who trust and delight in him (John 1:9–10; 8:12).

This is the God who sovereignly rules all of history and is bringing it to its consummation in Jesus Christ. What a marvelous and glorious thing! When we believe in him, there is no reason to fear and every reason to confidently rejoice as we look forward to eternal fellowship with God in heaven.

APPENDIX 1

HOW TO INTERACT
PERSONALLY WITH ATHEISTS

We have spent considerable time analyzing Dawkins's main beliefs and arguments. However, unlike many of the others treated in this Great Thinkers series, the primary exposure to Dawkins occurs, not through the written word, but through personal interactions. Speaking with a follower of Richard Dawkins is different from interacting with a series of words on a page. Therefore, we want to consider some pointers for conversing with atheists that you may encounter.

Interacting with a Person

Remember, you are talking with a person, not just a set of logical or illogical assumptions and beliefs. People are more than the sum of their beliefs. Everyone you talk to has been influenced and shaped by their history as well as an active heart, soul, and feelings (even if some may seem robotic or detached). Christianity is more than just right information achieved through a series of mental exercises, philosophical proofs, or logical syllogisms. It has to affect one's heart. "For with the heart one believes and is justified, and with the mouth one confesses and is saved" (Rom. 10:10). Christianity is a relationship with Christ that can be embodied at least partly through our relationship with others. We can win an argument and lose the person if we do not treat someone properly. *How* we say something can sometimes be as important as *what* we say. If what we say is not matching up with how we say it, then we can expect people to turn away.

Love

Much of this book focuses on truth, but we lose sight of the gospel when we wield truth like a weapon. We are not better because we know the truth. If it were not for God's grace, we would be equally resistant and deserving of God's justice. God calls us to testify to the truth, but to do so with love (Eph. 4:13). This means that, first and foremost, you need to love the person in front of you. Demonstrate that you are interested in and care about the person, not just his or her beliefs. Being a loving Christian means you are willing to listen, ask questions, and genuinely try to understand the person you are speaking with. This calls for humility, gentleness, and self-control. An angry or condescending tone is not loving (Prov. 29:11; James 1:19–20). It is loving to consider an individual's background and to be sensitive to their unique situation. Many people are angry at God for deeply personal reasons.[1] When we ignore a person's background and context, we are more likely to be just a banging gong that causes migraines (1 Cor. 13:1). We do not want to hinder the winsome nature of the gospel; we aim to highlight its attractiveness.

1. Elizabeth Landau, "Anger at God Common, Even among Atheists," *CNN*, January 1, 2011. Accessed online at http://thechart.blogs.cnn.com/2011/01/01 /anger-at-god-common-even-among-atheists/.

Holy Spirit

Finally, remember that no matter how "good" you are at debating, the person with whom you are speaking still needs the Holy Spirit. Souls are not won by slick rhetoric or even by compassionate, loving words. People enter the kingdom when God calls them and opens their heart to be receptive to his truth. Even if you say and do everything right, if God is not at work, it will be to no avail. On the flip side, no matter how "bad" you are at saying things, the Holy Spirit can use you (1 Cor. 3:6). Even if you "bungle" a discussion, work done for the glory of God in faith is good work. You are not a success or failure based on any humanly measurable outcome. Gifts offered to the Lord are judged by the attitude with which they are given. Just like the two small coins offered by the widow in Luke 21:1–4, even small gifts, given in love, have great meaning.

In the end, Dawkins could say that his beliefs might be incorrect, but he has no reason to believe that to be so, and it seems easier to him to remain an atheist than to posit something supernatural. Basically, Christianity might be true, but he does not want to believe it. In fact, I actually had a friend say this to me once. He did not want to surrender his autonomy. In those cases, we do not give up, but pray for God's work in their lives.

Overall Strategy

In what follows, I am going to briefly outline a conversational style known as presuppositional apologetics.

Step 1: Define Worldviews

Apologetic discussion begins with acknowledging that we have different worldviews, and see the world through different lenses. We may make the same observations, but draw completely different conclusions from them. If in fact we see things completely differently, how can there be any common ground for discussion?

"We are not trying to lead people to come to know a God who is completely new to them. Rather, we show that scientists *already know* God as an aspect of their human experience in the scientific enterprise.... The denial of God springs ultimately not from intellectual flaws or from failure to see all the way to the conclusion of a chain of syllogistic reasoning, but from spiritual failure. We are rebels against God, and we will not serve him."[2] The gospel "with its message of forgiveness and reconciliation through Christ, offers the only remedy that can truly end this fight against God."[3] We need to keep this in mind as we converse with others. If not for the grace of God, we would be in much the same position as our non-Christian friends.

As Christians, we believe that everyone has the knowledge of God in their hearts—they just choose to deny him (Rom. 1:18–32). So, there is a disconnect between what atheists say they believe (professed beliefs) and how they actually live (functional beliefs). For example, I might profess that the world is an illusion, but I deny that belief functionally because I do not randomly walk out on highways or step off cliffs. Similarly, atheists profess not to believe in God, but functionally they rely on him to live and make decisions.[4] In fact, Christianity explains why scientists can do science successfully while claiming to disbelieve in God.

Step 2: Find Worldview Disconnect

In order to demonstrate this, you must first find the point of disconnect and reveal it to the atheist. This means putting

2. Vern Poythress, *Redeeming Science: A God-Centered Approach* (Wheaton, IL: Crossway Books, 2006), 28.

3. Ibid., 29.

4. The very words and breath Dawkins uses to deny God have been gifted to him by God. ". . . since he himself gives to all mankind life and breath and everything" (Acts 17:25b).

yourself in the other person's shoes and *showing* them that their functional beliefs are not consistent with their professed beliefs. One common way of doing this is to examine underlying assumptions and the justification for them.

For example, an atheist may either (1) profess that there is no right and wrong, no morality, but then behave in a moral way (or expect others to do so), (2) behave morally and define right and wrong, but then have no justification (according to his own worldview) for behaving and believing in such a way, or (3) make moral judgments about others without justification. Sometimes you can help them see the logical conclusion of their worldview, such as ultimate despair, meaninglessness, or chaos.

This step in particular requires care, tenderness, and humility. Admitting to a philosophical inconsistency that undermines one's entire worldview is a scary proposition. This may just be the most difficult stage in your conversation with them. When people wrestle with this point, it is important to let them explore it on their own. Let them ask questions. Give them space to think. We are not here to force-feed truth in an unloving way.

Step 3: Demonstrate Christian Coherence and Harmony

Once this has been done, the Christian then invites the nonbeliever to consider the Christian perspective regarding the issue under consideration. Invite them, for the sake of argument, to imagine they are a Christian. Then point out that Christianity is more compelling, more comprehensive, and provides a more satisfactory explanation of the evidence. We have justification. We have a better story. We have a coherent truth. For example, Christianity explains why humans are here, why the world looks designed, and how to distinguish between good and evil.[5]

5. Now, we have greatly oversimplified the process and only addressed the logical rationale of a discussion. For a more thorough explanation of presuppositional apologetics, see *Christian Apologetics*, by Cornelius Van Til, or *Apologetics: A Justification*

Final Advice

Do not let others set the terms and box you into a definitional corner. Do not be afraid to ask what exactly someone means by a word. If they are misdefining it, work to clarify. If you agree with them about something, let them know. If they claim you believe something that you do not, make that clear.

Admit when you do not know or do not understand something. Ask for time. As finite beings, sometimes we need a break. We can say, "That is a great point. Let me think about that overnight and I will get back to you" (if this option is available to you). It is OK if you do not have all the answers. Remember, because God is transcendent, we cannot fully understand him, but because he is immanent, we can truly understand him.

For example, while we do not fully understand the existence of evil and suffering, we do know that God is not absent. We cannot say that God does not care, yet atheism says that nature does not care. Based on what we see in the Bible (Jesus entering this world to vanquish sin and death), God clearly cares and has promised justice, peace, and renewal, which is more than atheism can offer.[6]

Keep your emotions in check. Although we have confidence in God's truth, you will never browbeat someone into philosophical submission with heavy-handed logic and a hot temper. The Bible has stern warnings about anger (Eph. 4:31; James 1:19–20). Think about how you would like others to converse with you, and then treat them in the same way (Matt. 7:12).

Finally, pray. Then pray some more. Trust the ever-present Helper, your interceding Lord Jesus Christ, your sovereign and loving Father God.

---

of Christian Belief, by John Frame.

6. Timothy Keller, *The Reason for God: Belief in an Age of Skepticism* (New York: Dutton, 2008), chap. 2.

APPENDIX 2

FOR FURTHER READING

The following books are recommended for further reading.

Behe, Michael. *Darwin's Black Box: The Biochemical Challenge to Evolution*. New York: Free Press, 2006. An introduction to some of the difficulties for standard evolutionary theory to account for complex molecular structures.

———. *The Edge of Evolution: The Search for the Limits of Darwinism*. New York: Free Press, 2007. A discussion of the limits of change and adaptation that organisms are capable of (i.e., micro- vs. macroevolution).

Frame, John. *Apologetics: A Justification of Christian Belief*. Phillipsburg, NJ: P&R Publishing, 2015. An in-depth overview of a Christian approach to sharing and defending your faith.

Gilson, Tom, and Carson Weitnauer, eds., *True Reason: Confronting the Irrationality of the New Atheism*. Grand Rapids: Kregel Publications, 2014. A compilation of articles by several top thinkers reacting to the works of the New Atheists by discussing the flaws of materialism and naturalism.

Keller, Timothy. *The Reason for God: Belief in an Age of Skepticism.* New York: Dutton, 2008. A highly accessible discussion for lay readers on some common challenges to Christian belief.

Lennox, John. *God's Undertaker: Has Science Buried God?* Oxford: Lion Hudson, 2009. An excellent discussion of some of the new scientific evidence for God.

———. *Gunning for God: Why the New Atheists Are Missing the Target.* Oxford: Lion Hudson, 2011. An excellent treatise directly interacting with Dawkins and the New Atheists.

Lewis, C. S. *Miracles.* New York: HarperCollins, 1996. An introduction to miracles and how they fit into our world.

———. *Mere Christianity.* New York: HarperCollins, 1980. A very good, almost autobiographical primer on an apologetic for Christian belief.

McGrath, Alister. *Dawkins' God: Genes, Memes and the Meaning of Life.* Malden, MA: Blackwell Publishing, 2005. A good resource that interacts directly with the arguments that Dawkins makes.

Meyer, Stephen. *Signature in the Cell: DNA and the Evidence for Intelligent Design.* New York: HarperOne, 2009. An introduction to some of the difficulties for standard evolutionary theory to explain the origin of life.

———. *Darwin's Doubt: The Explosive Origin of Animal Life and the Case for Intelligent Design.* New York: HarperOne, 2014. An introduction to some of the difficulties for standard evolutionary theory to explain the complexity of life.

Moreland, J. P., and William Lane Craig. *Philosophical Foundations for a Christian Worldview.* 2nd edition. Downers Grove, IL: IVP Academic, 2017. A more philosophical introduction to the construction of a Christian worldview.

Poythress, Vern. *Redeeming Science: A God-Centered Approach.* Wheaton, IL: Crossway Books, 2006. An excellent introduction to how worldview affects the sciences and how we integrate our relationship with God into our pursuit of science.

Stokes, Mitch. *How to Be an Atheist: Why Many Skeptics Aren't Skeptical Enough.* Wheaton, IL: Crossway, 2016. A philosophical investigation into the inconsistencies of the New Atheists, with a specific emphasis on the problem of morality.

Van Til, Cornelius. *Christian Apologetics*. Edited by William Edgar. Phillipsburg, NJ: P&R Publishing, 2003. An excellent introduction to, and overview of, how to share and defend the Christian faith.

GLOSSARY

Adaptation. Generally, the process by which something (usually a living organism) adjusts to become better suited to a particular challenge, environment, or situation. Adaptations can be learned behaviors or changes at the genetic level.

Amino Acids. Twenty different molecules, regularly occurring in nature, that are incorporated into specific sequences (from less than 100 to more than 30,000) to make functional, three-dimensionally folded proteins. Errors in the sequencing of amino acids can lead to nonfolding or nonfunctional proteins, which can be fatal for an organism.

Atheism. A broad term that, at the most basic level, refers to a belief that there is no supernatural God. See chapter 4 for more.

Big Bang Theory. A theory stating that the universe originated as a "singularity" approximately 14 billion years ago, inflated rapidly, and has expanded to its current state at this time.

DNA. Deoxyribonucleic acid, the underlying genetic material in an organism that is passed onto the progeny. The DNA molecule consists of a long backbone chain of sugar phosphates, and the variation comes in the changing sequence of four nucleotide bases that branch off the backbone: adenine, cytosine, guanine, and thymine.

Evolution. A controversial term that can take on a variety of meanings, depending on the context. Most generally, it refers to change over time, but there is a wide range of qualifiers that can be applied as well. Charles Darwin popularized the term to describe his theory for how living organisms develop and change over time. For more, see chapter 7.

Fine-Tuning Argument. An argument that draws on the special circumstances and uncanny precision of the balance, order, and harmony of the universe and its physical constants to argue that the universe was specially designed. Without a designer, it is probabilistically extremely unlikely that we would have arrived at a universe that supports life at all. See chapter 7 for more.

Gene. Generally, a discrete packet of inherited material. One gene usually refers to the entire section of DNA that codes and gives instructions for a single, complete protein.

Genetics. The study of DNA and how inherited material is passed from one generation to the next and how it affects our development.

Intelligent Design. A movement of the last several decades that seeks to examine scientific arguments for intelligent causation of certain aspects of our universe. It frequently makes use of the logic of "inference to the best explanation"—that is, trying to determine the best explanation among several possible explanations for an observation.

Irreducible Complexity. An idea proposed in the late 1990s by Michael Behe that there exist certain molecular structures or processes that could not have been the product of slow, gradual, random evolutionary processes, since no functional intermediates exist and such intermediates are demanded for a random, gradualistic process to have any reasonable chance of arriving at an advantageous endpoint.

Junk DNA. A largely antiquated term referring to the apparent uselessness of large chunks of our genetic material that are not being used to make protein. Recent advances in molecular biology have demonstrated that much, if not all, of this material is useful. Although it is not directly responsible for the exact instructions for making protein, it is involved in regulating processes like how much, how fast, and how often protein gets made.

Miracle. A violation of our expectation of natural law that is still in keeping with God's providential plan and power. See chapter 9 for more.

Molecule. A single chemical unit composed of a series of atoms bonded together by strong electrochemical attractions. For example, a water molecule consists of two hydrogen atoms bound to a single oxygen atom.

Multiverse. The theory that our universe is just one of many universes (possibly infinitely many). It is sometimes offered as an answer to the fine-tuning argument; however, there is no scientific evidence to support this theory, and it is difficult to imagine any way to obtain such evidence. See chapter 7 for more.

Mutation. Refers to a change, usually in the DNA, although we sometimes discuss mutation at other levels of the cell, such as in protein. Often changes are deleterious—that is, they harm the organism. Some mutations are silent, having no apparent effect, and very few mutations can be beneficial in particular circumstances. Mutations most commonly occur due to random errors in copying DNA or other cellular processes. Some mutations are introduced by exogenous factors, such as ultraviolet radiation from sunlight and cancer-causing drugs.

Natural Selection. The process by which organisms that are better suited or adapted to a particular environment, situation, or challenge are more likely to succeed, survive, and pass on their genes to future generations. It is colloquially known as "survival of the fittest."

Naturalism. Roughly speaking, the idea that "nature" is all there is. There is no supernatural. Although there are distinctions, for the sake of this volume I have lumped this term in with a variety of other similar terms. See chapter 6 for more.

Nature. The physical aspect of the world. It is theoretically discernible and testable by humans and the scientific method.

New Atheism. A popular movement within atheism launched in the early twenty-first century by a series of books written by several outspoken individuals expressing a great deal of antagonism toward religion. See chapter 1 for more.

Religion. A systematic belief system that underlies value decisions and other choices about everyday life. Some definitions will confine religion to belief systems that involve the supernatural. See chapter 4 for more.

Science. The systematic study of the world we live in, usually with particular emphasis on the natural world. This usage can become fuzzy, depending on how one defines the natural world. If consciousness is outside of the natural world, for example, the inclusion of a discipline like psychology can be challenging. Even the study of the natural world, as done by a conscious mind, can have an effect on how systematic the study is. See chapter 6 for more.

Scientific Method. A systematic, procedural approach to the sciences that involves observation, hypothesis, experimentation, measurement, data collection and analysis, and conclusions. When possible, the steps are repeated at least three times for any given experiment, in order to ensure the consistency, accuracy, and statistical significance of the results.

Supernatural. Something that exists outside the confines of a purely materialistic perspective. It is not reducible simply to matter and motion.

Worldview. The perspective with which an individual approaches, views, and analyzes the world. It affects every aspect of living, including conscious and unconscious value decisions. See chapter 6 for more.

BIBLIOGRAPHY

Aarts, A. A., et al. "Estimating the Reproducibility of Psychological Science." *Science* 349, no. 6251 (August 28, 2015). Accessed online at http://science.sciencemag.org/content/349/6251/aac 4716.

Alberts, Bruce, Alexander D. Johnson, et al. *Molecular Biology of the Cell.* 6th edition. New York: Garland Science, 2014.

Anderson, Elizabeth. "If God Is Dead, Is Everything Permitted?" In *The Portable Atheist,* edited by Christopher Hitchens. Philadelphia: Da Capo Press, 2007.

Appiah, Kwame Anthony. "Science Knows Best." *New York Times,* October 1, 2010. Accessed online at http://www.nytimes.com /2010/10/03/books/review/Appiah-t.html.

Atkins, Peter. *Nature's Imagination: The Frontiers of Scientific Vision.* Edited by John Cornwell. Oxford: Oxford University Press, 1995.

Axe, Douglas D. "The Case against a Darwinian Origin of Protein Folds." *BIO-Complexity* 1 (2010): 1–12.

———. *Undeniable: How Biology Confirms Our Intuition That Life Is Designed.* New York: HarperOne, 2016.

Baggini, Julian. *Atheism—A Very Short Introduction.* Oxford: Oxford University Press, 2003.

Bavinck, Herman. *In the Beginning: Foundations of Creation Theology.* Grand Rapids: Baker, 1999.

Behe, M. J. "Experimental Evolution, Loss-of-Function Mutations, and the 'First Rule of Adaptive Evolution.'" *Quarterly Review of Biology* 85, no. 4 (December 2010): 419–45.

Behe, Michael. *Darwin's Black Box: The Biochemical Challenge to Evolution.* New York: Free Press, 2006.

———. *The Edge of Evolution: The Search for the Limits of Darwinism.* New York: Free Press, 2007.

Berlinski, David. *The Devil's Delusion: Atheism and Its Scientific Pretensions.* New York: Crown Forum, 2008.

Blanco, Francisco, Isabelle Angrand, and Luis Serrano. "Exploring the Conformational Properties of the Sequence Space between Two Proteins with Different Folds: An Experimental Study." *Journal of Molecular Biology* 285, no. 2 (January 1999): 741–53.

Bloom, John. *The Natural Sciences: A Student's Guide.* Wheaton, IL: Crossway, 2015.

Blount, Z. D., J. E. Barrick, C. J. Davidson, and R. E Lenski. "Genomic Analysis of a Key Innovation in an Experimental Escherichia coli Population." *Nature* 489, no. 7417 (September 2012): 513–18.

Blount, Zachary D., Christina Z. Borland, and Richard E. Lenski. "Historical Contingency and the Evolution of a Key Innovation in an Experimental Population of Escherichia coli." *Proceedings of the National Academy of Sciences of the United States of America* 105, no. 23 (June 2008): 7899–906.

Boolos, George. "Gödel's Second Incompleteness Theorem Explained in Words of One Syllable." *Mind* 103 (1994): 1–3.

Brian, Denis. *The Voice of Genius: Conversations with Nobel Scientists and Other Luminaries.* New York: Basic Books, 2000.

Bridgham, Jamie T., Sean M. Carrol, and Joseph W. Thornton. "Evolution of Hormone-Receptor Complexity by Molecular Exploitation." *Science* 32, no. 5770 (April 7, 2006): 97–101. Accessed online at http://science.sciencemag.org/content/312/5770/97.

Brooks, David. "The Age of Darwin." *New York Times*, April 15, 2007,

WK14. Accessed online at http://www.nytimes.com/2007/04/15/opinion/15brooks.html?_r=0.

Burns, K., and A. Bechara. "Decision Making and Free Will: A Neuroscience Perspective." *Behavioral Sciences and the Law*, 25, no. 2 (2007): 263–80.

Churchland, Patricia Smith. "Epistemology in the Age of Neuroscience." *The Journal of Philosophy* 84, no. 10 (October 1987): 544–53.

Collins, Francis. *The Language of God: A Scientist Presents Evidence for Belief*. New York: Free Press, 2006.

Collins, Robin. "A Scientific Argument for the Existence of God: The Fine-Tuning Design Argument." In *Reason for the Hope Within*, edited by Michael J. Murray, 47–75. Grand Rapids: Eerdmans, 1999.

Craig, William Lane. "The Existence of God and the Beginning of the Universe." *Truth: A Journal of Modern Thought* 3 (1991): 85–96. Accessed online at http://www.leaderu.com/truth/3truth11.html.

Cronin, Leroy, and Sara Imari Walker. "Beyond Prebiotic Chemistry." *Science* 352, no. 6290 (June 3, 2016): 1174–75. Accessed online at http://science.sciencemag.org/content/352/6290/1174.full.

Davies, Paul. *The Mind of God: The Scientific Basis for a Rational World*. New York: Simon & Schuster, 1992.

Dawkins, Richard. *An Appetite for Wonder: The Making of a Scientist*. London: Bantam, 2013.

———. *Brief Candle in the Dark: My Life in Science*. London: Bantam, 2015.

———. *The Blind Watchmaker*. New York: W. W. Norton, 1986.

———. *Climbing Mount Improbable*. New York: W. W. Norton, 1996.

———. In *Daily Telegraph Science Extra*, September 11, 1989.

———. *A Devil's Chaplain: Reflections on Hope, Lies, Science, and Love*. New York: Mariner Books, 2003.

———. "Foreword." In *God, the Devil, and Darwin: A Critique of Intelligent Design Theory*, by Niall Shanks. New York: Oxford University Press, 2004.

———. "From the Afterword." *The Herald Scotland*, November 20,

2006. Accessed online at http://www.heraldscotland.com/news /12760676.From_the_Afterword/.

———. *The God Delusion*. New York: Houghton Mifflin, 2006, 2008.

———. *The Greatest Show on Earth*. New York: Free Press, 2009.

———. "Is Science a Religion?" *The Humanist*, January-February, 1997, 26–39.

———. "The Ontogeny of a Pecking Preference in Domestic Chicks." *Zeitschrift für Tierpsychologie* 25 (1968): 170–86.

———. "Richard Dawkins Review of Blueprints: Solving the Mystery of Evolution." *New York Times*, April 9, 1989, section 7. Accessed online at http://www.philvaz.com/apologetics/p88.htm.

———. *River out of Eden: A Darwinian View of Life*. New York: Basic Books, 1995.

———. *The Selfish Gene*. Oxford: Oxford University Press, 1976.

———. "A Survival Machine." In *The Third Culture*, edited by John Brockman. New York: Simon & Schuster, 1996.

———. *Unweaving the Rainbow: Science, Delusion, and the Appetite for Wonder*. New York: Mariner Books, 1998.

Dawkins, Richard, and Yan Wong. *The Ancestor's Tale: A Pilgrimage to the Dawn of Evolution*. Revised edition. New York: Mariner Books, 2016.

de Oliveira, Cleuci. "The Right to Kill." *Foreign Policy*, April 9, 2018. Accessed online at https://foreignpolicy.com/2018/04/09/the -right-to-kill-brazil-infanticide/.

Dennett, Daniel. *Breaking the Spell: Religion as a Natural Phenomenon*. London: Penguin Books, 2006.

Derbyshire, Jonathan. "Richard Dawkins Was No 1. Now He's off the List of the World's Best Thinkers." *The Guardian*, March 22, 2014. Accessed online at https://www.theguardian.com/commentis free/2014/mar/22/goodbye-richard-dawkins-hail-pope-francis -prospect-magazine.

Dowe, Phil. *Galileo, Darwin, and Hawking*. Grand Rapids, MI: Eerdmans Publishing Company, 2005.

Earman, John. *Hume's Abject Failure: The Argument Against Miracles*. New York: Oxford University Press, 2000.

Ecklund, Elaine Howard. *Science vs. Religion: What Scientists Really Think*. Oxford: Oxford University Press, 2010.

Einstein, Albert. "Physics and Reality" (1936). In *Ideas and Opinions*, translated by Sonja Bargmann. New York: Bonanza, 1954.

Elmhirst, Sophie. "Is Richard Dawkins Destroying His Reputation?" *The Guardian*, June 9, 2015. Accessed online at https://www.theguardian.com/science/2015/jun/09/is-richard-dawkins-destroying-his-reputation.

Epstein, Greg. *Good without God: What a Billion Nonreligious People Do Believe*. New York: HarperCollins, 2009.

Esfandiar, Joseph, and Hannon Bozorgmehr. "Is Gene Duplication a Viable Explanation for the Origination of Biological Information and Complexity?" *Complexity* 16, no. 6 (2011): 17–31.

Espinoza, Javier. "All Pupils at Non-faith Schools Must Study Atheism, Judge Rules." *The Telegraph*, November 25, 2015. Accessed online at http://www.telegraph.co.uk/education/12015859/Non-religious-views-should-not-have-been-left-out-of-new-GCSE-High-Court-rules.html.

Evans, John H. "Does Science Undermine Human Rights?" *New Scientist*, August 3, 2016. Accessed online at https://www.newscientist.com/article/mg23130850-200-who-we-think-we-are-and-why-it-matters/.

Frame, John. *Apologetics: A Justification of Christian Belief*. Phillipsburg, NJ: P&R Publishing, 2015.

———. *The Doctrine of the Word of God*. Phillipsburg, NJ: P&R Publishing, 2010.

Frankl, Viktor. *Man's Search for Meaning*. Boston: Beacon Press, 2006.

Furness, Hannah. "Richard Dawkins: Churchgoers Enable Fundamentalists by Being 'Nice'." *The Telegraph*, August 13, 2014. Accessed online at http://www.telegraph.co.uk/news/religion/11032654/Richard-Dawkins-Churchgoers-enable-fundamentalists-by-being-nice.html.

Gilson, Tom, and Carson Weitnauer, eds. *True Reason: Confronting the Irrationality of the New Atheism*. Grand Rapids: Kregel Publications, 2014.

Hacking, Ian. "The Inverse Gambler's Fallacy: The Argument from Design. The Anthropic Principle Applied to Wheeler Universes." *Mind* 96 (1987): 331–40.

Harold, Franklin M. *The Way of the Cell: Molecules, Organisms, and the Order of Life.* New York: Oxford University Press, 2001.

Harris, Sam. *The End of Faith: Religion, Terror, and the Future of Reason.* New York: W. W. Norton, 2004.

———. *Free Will.* New York: Free Press, 2012.

———. *The Moral Landscape: How Science Can Determine Human Values.* New York: Free Press, 2010.

———. "Toward a Science of Morality." *The Huffington Post,* July 6, 2010. Accessed online at http://www.huffingtonpost.com/sam -harris/a-science-of-morality_b_567185.html.

Haught, John F. *God and the New Atheism.* Louisville: Westminster John Knox, 2008.

Hawking, Stephen, and Leonard Mlodinow. *The Grand Design.* New York: Bantam, 2010.

Hedges, Chris. *I Don't Believe in Atheists.* New York: Free Press, 2008.

Hitchens, Christopher. *God Is Not Great.* New York: Twelve Books, 2007.

Holden, Michael. "God Did Not Create the Universe, Says Hawking." *Reuters,* September 2, 2010. Accessed online at: https://www .reuters.com/article/us-britain-hawking/god-did-not-create -the-universe-says-hawking-idUSTRE6811FN20100902

Hottes, Alison K., Peter L. Freddolino, Anupama Khare, Zachary N. Donnell, Julia C. Liu, and Saeed Tavazoie. "Bacterial Adaptation through Loss of Function." *PLoS Genetics* 9(7), July 2013, 1–13. Accessed online at https://www.ncbi.nlm.nih.gov/pmc/articles /PMC3708842/.

Hume, David. *An Enquiry concerning Human Understanding.* Indianapolis: Hackett Publishing, 1993.

———. *A Treatise of Human Nature.* Oxford: Clarendon, 1978.

Humphrey, Nicholas. "What Shall We Tell the Children?" In *The Values of Science: Oxford Amnesty Lectures,* edited by W. Williams. Boulder, CO: Westview, 1998.

Huxley, Aldous. *Ends and Means: An Inquiry into the Nature of Ideas and into the Methods Employed for Their Realization.* New York: Harper & Brothers, 1937.

Johnson, George. "A Free-for-All on Science and Religion." *New York Times*, November 21, 2006. Accessed online at http://www.nytimes.com/2006/11/21/science/21belief.html?_r=1.

Johnson, Phillip E., and John Mark Reynolds. *Against All Gods: What's Right and Wrong about the New Atheism.* Downers Grove, IL: InterVarsity Press, 2010.

Kato et al. "Amino Acid Alterations Essential for Increasing the Catalytic Activity of the Nylon-Oligomer-Degradation Enzyme of Favobacterium Sp." *European Journal of Biochemistry* 200, no. 1 (August 15, 1991): 165–69.

Keller, Timothy. *The Reason for God: Belief in an Age of Skepticism.* New York: Dutton, 2008.

Kimura, Motoo. *The Neutral Theory of Molecular Evolution.* Cambridge: Cambridge University Press, 1983.

Koonin, Eugene. *The Logic of Chance: The Nature and Origin of Biological Evolution.* Upper Saddle River, NJ: FT Press, 2011.

Kuyper, Abraham. *Abraham Kuyper: A Centennial Reader.* Edited by James D. Bratt. Grand Rapids: Eerdmans, 1998.

Labin, A. M., S. K. Safuri, E. N. Ribak, and I. Perlman. "Müller Cells Separate between Wavelengths to Improve Day Vision with Minimal Effect upon Night Vision." *Nature Communications* 5 (July 8, 2014): 4319.

Lamb, Trevor D., Shaun P. Collin, and Edward N. Pugh Jr. "Evolution of the Vertebrate Eye: Opsins, Photoreceptors, Retina, and Eye Cup." *Nature Reviews Neuroscience* 8, no. 12 (December 8, 2007): 960–76. Accessed online at https://www.ncbi.nlm.nih.gov/pmc/articles/PMC3143066/.

Landau, Elizabeth. "Anger at God Common, Even among Atheists." *CNN*, January 1, 2011. Accessed online at http://thechart.blogs.cnn.com/2011/01/01/anger-at-god-common-even-among-atheists/.

Lee, Adam. "Richard Dawkins has lost it: ignorant sexism gives atheists a bad name." *The Guardian*, September 18, 2014.

Lennox, John. *God's Undertaker: Has Science Buried God?* Oxford: Lion
Hudson, 2009.

———. *Gunning for God: Why the New Atheists Are Missing the Target.*
Oxford: Lion Hudson, 2011.

Lewis, C. S. *Miracles*. 1947; New York: HarperCollins, 1996.

Lewontin, Richard. "Billions and Billions of Demons." *New York Times
Book Review*, January 9, 1997, 31.

Lipton, Peter. "Inference to the Best Explanation." In *A Companion
to the Philosophy of Science*, edited by W. H. Newton-Smith.
Malden, MA: Blackwell Publishing, 2000.

MacCluskie, Kathryn C., and R. Elliott Ingersoll. *Becoming a
21st Century Agency Counselor*. Belmont, CA: Brooks/Cole
Counseling, 2001.

Marshall, David. *The Truth behind the New Atheism: Responding to
the Emerging Challenges to God and Christianity*. Eugene, OR:
Harvest House Publishers, 2007.

McGrath, Alister. *Dawkins' God: Genes, Memes and the Meaning of Life.*
Malden, MA: Blackwell Publishing, 2005.

———. *Why God Won't Go Away*. Nashville: Thomas Nelson, 2010.

McGrath, Alister E., and Joanna Collicutt McGrath. *The Dawkins
Delusion?* Downers Grove, IL: InterVarsity Press, 2007.

Meyer, Stephen. *Darwin's Doubt: The Explosive Origin of Animal Life
and the Case for Intelligent Design*. New York: HarperOne, 2014.

———. *Signature in the Cell: DNA and the Evidence for Intelligent
Design*. New York: HarperOne, 2009.

Miller, Boaz. "When Is Consensus Knowledge Based? Distinguishing
Shared Knowledge from Mere Agreement." *Synthese*, 190, no. 7
(May 2013).

Mish, Frederick, ed. *Merriam-Webster's Collegiate Dictionary*. 10th edition. Springfield, MA: Merriam-Webster, 2000.

Mukhopadhyay, Rajendrani. "Close to a Miracle." *ASBMB Today* 12,
no. 9 (October 2013): 12–13.

Müller, Gerd B. "Why an Extended Evolutionary Synthesis Is

Necessary." *Interface Focus* 7 (2017): 20170015. Accessed online at http://rsfs.royalsocietypublishing.org/content/roy focus/7/5/20170015.full.pdf.

Nagel, Thomas. "The Fear of Religion." *The New Republic*, October 23, 2006.

Nickerson, Raymond S. "Confirmation Bias: A Ubiquitous Phenomenon in Many Guises." *Review of General Psychology* 2, no. 2 (June 1998): 175–220.

Onfray, Michel. *Atheist Manifesto: The Case against Christianity, Judaism, and Islam.* New York: Arcade Publishing, 2005.

Paley, William. *Natural Theology; or Evidences of the Existence and Attributes of the Deity.* 18th edition. Edinburgh: James Sawers, 1818.

Pearcey, Nancy, and Charles Thaxton. *The Soul of Science: Christian Faith and Natural Philosophy.* Wheaton, IL: Crossway, 1994.

Peterson, Gregory R. "Demarcation and the Scientistic Fallacy." *Zygon: Journal of Religion and Science* 38 (December 9, 2003): 751–61.

Peterson, Michael, William Hasker, Bruce Reichenback, and David Basinger, eds. *Philosophy of Religion.* 3rd edition. Oxford: Oxford University Press, 2007.

Plantinga, Alvin. *Where the Conflict Really Lies.* Oxford: Oxford University Press, 2011.

Poythress, Vern. *Chance and the Sovereignty of God: A God-Centered Approach to Probability and Random Events.* Wheaton, IL: Crossway, 2014.

———. *Inerrancy and Worldview: Answering Modern Challenges to the Bible.* Wheaton, IL: Crossway, 2012.

———. *Redeeming Science: A God-Centered Approach.* Wheaton, IL: Crossway Books, 2006.

Rae, Scott B. *Doing the Right Thing: Making Moral Choices in a World Full of Options.* Grand Rapids, MI: Zondervan, 2013.

Rosenberg, Alexander. *The Atheist's Guide to Reality: Enjoying Life without Illusions.* New York: W. W. Norton, 2011.

Ross, Hugh. "Anthropic Principle: A Precise Plan for Humanity." *Reasons to Believe,* January 1, 2002. Accessed online at http://www.reasons .org/articles/anthropic-principle-a-precise-plan-for-humanity.

Rossiter, Wayne. *Shadow of Oz*. Eugene, OR: Pickwick Publications, 2015.

Ruse, Michael, and Edward O. Wilson. "Evolution and Ethics." *New Scientist* 108 (October 17, 1985): 50–52.

Russell, Bertrand. "A Free Man's Worship." In *Mysticism and Logic and Other Essays*. Charleston, SC: BiblioLife, 2010.

———. *Religion and Science*. Oxford: Oxford University Press, 1970.

Russell, Bertrand, and Frederick Copleston. "Debate on the Existence of God." In *The Existence of God*, edited by John Hick. New York: Macmillan, 1964.

Sagan, Carl. *Pale Blue Dot: A Vision of the Human Future in Space*. New York: Random House, 1994.

Shermer, Michael. "How to Convince Someone When Facts Fail." *Scientific American*, January 1, 2017. Accessed online at https://www.scientificamerican.com/article/how-to-convince-someone-when-facts-fail/.

———. *Why Darwin Matters: The Case against Intelligent Design*. New York: Holt, 2006.

Sosa, Chris. "I'm Finally Breaking Up with Richard Dawkins." *The Huffington Post*, February 1, 2016. Accessed online at http://www.huffingtonpost.com/chris-sosa/im-finally-breaking-up-with-richard-dawkins_b_9102116.html.

Speed, David, Thomas Coleman II, and Joseph Langston. "What Do You Mean, 'What Does It All Mean?' Atheism, Nonreligion, and Life Meaning." *SAGE Open* 8 no. 1 (January 2018): 1–13.

Spetner, L. N. "Natural Selection versus Gene Uniqueness." *Nature* 226 (1970): 948–49.

Stenger, Victor. *God: The Failed Hypothesis*. Amherst, NY: Prometheus Books, 2007.

Stokes, Mitch. *How to Be an Atheist: Why Many Skeptics Aren't Skeptical Enough*. Wheaton, IL: Crossway, 2016.

Stone, Marcia. "For Microbes, Devolution Is Evolution." *BioScience* 64, no. 10 (October 2014): 956.

Sun, Eryn. "Former Dawkins Atheist Richard Morgan Continues to Praise God." *The Christian Post*, March 24, 2011. Accessed online at http://www.christianpost.com/news/former-dawkins-atheist -richard-morgan-continues-to-praise-god-49558/.

Torrance, Thomas. *Theological Science*. Edinburgh, UK: T&T Clark, 1996.

Urry, Lisa A., Michael L. Cain, et al. *Campbell Biology in Focus*. 2nd edition. New York: Pearson, 2015.

Van Biema, David. "God vs. Science." *Time*, November 5, 2006. Accessed online at http://content.time.com/time/magazine /article/0,9171,1555132,00.html.

Van Hofwegen, D. J., C. J. Hovde, and S. A. Minnich. "Rapid Evolution of Citrate Utilization by Escherichia coli by Direct Selection Requires citT and dctA." *Journal of Bacteriology* 198, no. 7 (February 2016): 1022–34.

Van Til, Cornelius. *Christian Apologetics*. Edited by William Edgar. Phillipsburg, NJ: P&R Publishing, 2003.

von Weizsäcker, C. F. *The Relevance of Science*. New York: Collins, 1964.

Ward, Keith. *Why There Almost Certainly Is a God*. Oxford: Lion Hudson, 2008.

Warfield, Benjamin Breckinridge. *The Inspiration and Authority of the Bible*. Phillipsburg, NJ: Presbyterian and Reformed, 1948.

Weikart, Richard. *The Death of Humanity: And the Case for Life*. Washington, DC: Regnery Faith, 2016.

———. *From Darwin to Hitler: Evolutionary Ethics, Eugenics, and Racism in Germany*. London: Palgrave Macmillan, 2006.

Wells, Jonathan. *Icons of Evolution*. Washington, DC: Regnery, 2000.

———. *The Myth of Junk DNA*. Seattle: Discovery Institute Press, 2011.

West, John. *Darwin Day in America*. Wilmington, DE: ISI Books, 2007.

Whitehead, Alfred North. *Science and the Modern World*. 1925; New York: Free Press, 1997.

Williams, Mary Elizabeth. "Stop Pouting, Richard Dawkins: Sharing a Rape 'Joke' Targeting an Activist Is a 'De-platforming' Offense." *Salon*, January 28, 2016. Accessed online at http://www.salon .com/2016/01/28/stop_pouting_richard_dawkins_sharing_a _rape_joke_targeting_an_activist_is_a_de_platforming_offense/.

Wirth, Alberto, Giuliano Cavallacci, and Frederica Genovesi-Ebert. "The Advantages of an Inverted Retina. A Physiological Approach to a Teleological Question." *Developments in Ophthalmology* 9 (1984): 20–28.

Wolf, Gary. "The Church of the Non-Believers." *Wired*, November 2006. Accessed online at https://www.wired.com/2006/11/atheism/.

Young, Edward J. *Thy Word Is Truth*. London: Banner of Truth, 1963.

Zax, David. "True Nonbeliever." *Yale Alumni Magazine*, July-August, 2016, 31–33.

INDEX OF SCRIPTURE

INDEX OF SUBJECTS AND NAMES

Ransom Poythress grew up in a home that encouraged a deep and robust harmonization of science and theology, based on a foundational Christian belief. His excitement about these topics carried him through the science fairs of the public-school system to a BS in biology at Caltech and on to a PhD in molecular and cell biology and biochemistry at Boston University. During those years, he was exposed to a wide variety of secular worldviews. He also began to perceive a degree of apprehension, timidity, and fear in Christian circles about the sciences, and this ultimately led him to Westminster Theological Seminary. There Poythress obtained his MA and learned how to compellingly and compassionately convey his enthusiasm about the underlying harmony of Christianity and science. All of this has contributed to his personal research interest in the philosophy of science and biblical apologetics: while upholding the sovereignty of God and the inerrancy of Scripture, how can we winsomely, knowledgeably, and lovingly use God's creation and our finite understanding of the sciences to effectively engage the culture? Poythress currently teaches biology at Houghton College, where he continues to pass along his passion for God and science to a new generation of scholar-servants. He and his wife, Lisbeth, live near the college, where they enjoy ministering to the students and playing board games and ultimate Frisbee.